Hints and Tips for Helping Children with Autism Spectrum Disorders

Useful Strategies for Home, School, and the Community

Dion E. Betts and Nancy J. Patrick

Jessica Kingsley Publishers
London and Philadelphia

First published in 2008
by Jessica Kingsley Publishers
116 Pentonville Road
London N1 9JB, UK
and
400 Market Street, Suite 400
Philadelphia, PA 19106, USA

www.jkp.com

Library of Congress Cataloging in Publication Data
Betts, Dion E. (Dion Emile), 1963-
   Hints and tips for helping children with autism spectrum disorders : useful strategies for
home, school, and the community / Dion E Betts and Nancy J. Patrick.
       p. cm.
   Includes bibliographical references.
   ISBN 978-1-84310-896-2 (pb : alk. paper) 1. Autistic children--Care. 2. Autistic
children--Education. 3. Parents of autistic children. I. Patrick, Nancy J. (Nancy Jo), 1955- II.
Title.
   RJ506.A9B448 2009
   649'.154--dc22

                                                          2008016777

British Library Cataloguing in Publication Data
A CIP catalogue record for this book is available from the British Library

ISBN 978 1 84310 896 2

Printed and bound in the United States by
Thomson-Shore, 7300 Joy Road, Dexter, MI 48130

Acknowledgements

We wish to thank the many parents with whom we have worked over the past twenty years. They have generously shared their stories about their lives and experiences with their children. They were honest about the frustrations and successes with children with autism spectrum disorders. Much of this book is our attempt to pass along the homespun remedies generated by these pioneers.

A note on the book

The information in this book is intended to be just one part in a comprehensive program of care for children with autism spectrum disorders that is provided by parents, caregivers, and educational, and medical professionals. The information in this book is not intended to "cure" these disorders. There is no cure for autism at this time. A medical examination by a physician for a child suspected of having an autism spectrum disorder and other possible disorders is essential.

Many children have additional medical problems in addition to their diagnosed autism spectrum disorder. Parents and caregivers are encouraged to consult with a physician before acting on some of the recommendations in this book.

Many of the stories in this book are based on the kinds of experiences that many families with children with autism spectrum disorders go through. Stories and recommendations are not based on word-for-word interviews. Rather, they are based on a culmination of the authors' experiences with children and families. Thus, any perceived depiction of actual individuals is purely coincidental.

Contents

Introduction: What is So Special about Children with Autism Spectrum Disorders?

Paula is now ten years old. She is a beautiful girl with long blonde hair and sparkling blue eyes. Her hair is lifted off her forehead by a cowlick just left of center, which gives her a fresh wind-blown look.

If you were to look at her in a photograph or watch her sleeping, you would think that she most assuredly would be a popular girl, maybe even the most popular girl in her class. I have often asked myself what makes a child popular among their peers or even allows them to make and keep friendships. I used to think that maybe it had something to do with the way you looked or the way you dressed, but I have come to learn that it is much more than that. My life with Paula has been a journey of getting to know my child, observing her living, seeing her struggles and then trying to create solutions for her deficits that would allow her to live a full and meaningful life.

I first realized that other children did not seem to warm to Paula when she was three years old. At that point, I made a concerted effort to have her attend playgroups, preschool, participate in soccer, and sing in the children's church choir. I was vigilant in getting reports from the people supervising each social encounter, so that I could repair any problem between Paula and the adults or children. Most of the infractions with adults had to do with her correcting them, which was interpreted as rude and sometimes defiant.

Most of the problems with the children involved insensitivity to their opinions and perspectives. This in many cases involved competing at inappropriate times, being bossy, not including their ideas in the playtime, and, in general, being quite self-centered. Occasionally

Paula would recognize a mistake or would acknowledge a cue from me that she had done something terribly wrong, but she did not know how to correct the problem on the spot to recoup the friendship, even when she had some awareness that a problem had arisen.

Over the years, the invitations to events and activities ceased. Other children occasionally responded positively to invitations to play, but even those play dates were infrequent. She still longed for friends even though almost every social situation ended on a negative note. Paula was far less distressed by the situations than her playmates. Paula begs for friends.

Finally, someone agreed to come and play with her. We talked about it. We planned. Paula and I previewed the day to ensure a successful event with the hope that this would be ongoing. The first thing she did was to compete with the child. Paula told her friend, "I bet I can swim across the pool faster than you can." She couldn't. Her friend looked at her, and was quiet and polite. She never called again.

Sarah, Paula's mom

Zach kept crying and yelling about having to come to dinner. He really freaked when I shut off the computer. He said, "You don't care about me, all you care about is the stupid dinner." I get him to sit for dinner and he sees that we are eating hotdogs. Zach cries and hits his hands on the table. My other kids yell back at him. Zach gets up to hit his brother. I say, "Ok, I'll make you some spaghetti." Zach then says he wants it with tomato sauce, not butter. I say okay. The other kids also want spaghetti now. The menu for everyone changed to spaghetti with tomato sauce. The hotdogs return to the refrigerator.

Frank, Zach's dad

Some people would say that these children are spoiled. However, their distress is real. It torments them and pervades all aspects of family life. This book is a collection of practical remedies for daily predicaments for children with autism spectrum disorders. It is a culmination of many families' experiences and their tried and true solutions to everything from bringing a child to the dentist to family vacations. What parents of children with autism spectrum disorders know is that their children are different. Many times they do not know why this is so. Parents and caregivers want to explain to friends and family why their child is different. They also want to know how to make the home and community more calm and joyful.

What are autism spectrum disorders?

Autism spectrum disorders are disorders of communication, being able to relate socially, and self-regulation in individuals of all ages. It is generally accepted that the underpinnings of autism spectrum disorders are central nervous system dysfunctions. However, there is disagreement in medical literature regarding the causes and treatment of autism spectrum disorders. Moreover, there is a dispute as to how to differentiate between autism spectrum disorders in making medical diagnoses. The diagnoses of Pervasive Developmental Disorder, Childhood Degenerative Disorder, autism, and Asperger Syndrome all are within the category of autism spectrum disorders.

Children with autism spectrum disorders frequently exhibit problems in the area of executive function. Executive function refers to the ability to connect past experiences with present action and is used to pay attention, sequence, strategize, memorize, organize, and retrieve information. Executive function is essential in planning and problem solving. Executive function also helps individuals manage and regulate emotions, including anger, in a socially appropriate manner. Children who have problems in executive function will have difficulty organizing and sequencing details, planning a project, sustaining and shifting attention, sensing time, and self-monitoring.

Executive functioning happens mostly in the frontal lobe of the brain. This area of the brain takes longer to develop compared with other parts of the brain. It is believed that the frontal lobe continues to develop late in adolescence and that there is a dramatic growth spurt between the ages of seventeen and twenty. Many researchers agree that the most likely cause of problems in executive function is a developmental impairment. Treatments include medication that addresses biochemical activity in the frontal lobe and behavioral and instructional interventions. Assessments and treatment recommendations by medical and other professionals are urged for children with autism spectrum disorders when these disabilities significantly impair functions of daily living.

Many children with autism have a type of mind blindness that prevents them from predicting how others will interpret and respond to their comments and behaviors. This area of difficulty is referred to as theory of mind and is defined as "the ability to recognize and understand the thoughts, beliefs, desires and intentions of other people in order to make sense of their behavior and predict what they are going to do next" (Attwood 2007). Major researchers have hypothesized that impairment in theory of mind, also defined by some as perspective-taking, is a core deficit of autism (Baron-Cohen 1989).

The weakness or inability to see a situation from the perspective of another child or adult can cause major misunderstandings that lead to considerable social problems. Some of the social problems arise from the child not being able to judge the appropriateness of comments and behaviors that might hurt someone's feelings or cause them to feel embarrassed. In this case the child's intentions are not to hurt or embarrass another person, but the child is not able to predict how the other person will perceive their comments or behavior. Conversations are also negatively affected since the speaker and listener in a conversation must be able to attend to the perspective of the other person in order for the conversation to flow smoothly. Other problems include the inability to interpret the feelings and nonverbal behaviors of others that prevent the child from quickly identifying a social misunderstanding so that some type of repair or fix-up strategy can be applied to avert a problem.

The strategies outlined in this book are designed to both support children with autism spectrum disorders and also to help them develop skills to manage and enjoy daily living. Behavior strategies are given and include creating checklists and "to do" lists, breaking down assignments into smaller segments and directions, and giving specific time frames for completion. Strategies explained also include using visual schedules and calendars, graphic and other organizers, and social scripts and mnemonics to support memory and retrieval. Tips for planning and structuring transition times are also given.

The purpose of this book is not to explore the controversy over the causes or diagnoses of autism spectrum disorders, but to illustrate ways of handling commonly experienced problems in individuals and families. Parents, professionals, and carers have many similar things to say about how difficult it is for children with autism spectrum disorders to get through most days. Experiences that are usually considered enjoyable are often traumatic for children with autism spectrum disorders. Parents, professionals, and carers are looking for ways to help these children get through the day and to help them enjoy life to the fullest.

Experiences of children with autism spectrum disorders

What is so difficult about raising a child with an autism spectrum disorder is that solely using a traditional approach to parenting often does not work very well. For example, setting rules and expectations alone or expecting a child to learn by watching others is not enough for many children with autism spectrum disorders to be successful in the home and community.

· We, as parents, have first-hand experience in this regard. Here is a situation Dion experienced:

> I remember that before our son was diagnosed with Asperger Syndrome, he would come home from kindergarten each day with a note about how poorly he behaved in school. He would lie on the classroom floor, become upset during assemblies, and refuse to follow simple teacher requests.
>
> I also remember getting calls at work from the school principal asking me to talk to my son about his school behavior. This approach did not help change his behavior. My wife and I were frustrated with the school and with our son because we didn't know what to do. Nothing seemed to work.
>
> Shortly thereafter, my son was assessed and diagnosed with Asperger Syndrome. Recommendations included speech therapy, social skills training, and a teacher assistant to work with our son in school. These were fine recommendations, but they were only the beginning of what our son really needed to function effectively at home, in the community, and at school.

What parents and caregivers need to know

Years of working with children with autism spectrum disorders and hours of interviews with parents and caregivers have convinced us and experts in the field that a traditional approach to dealing with behaviors (for example, by using solely rewards and consequences) will not help children with autism spectrum disorders reach their fullest potential.

When needed, medication can help support children as part of the learning process. Medication alone cannot give children the skills they need to get through the day. As an example, children with autism spectrum disorders need to learn how to hold an appropriate conversation with a friend. Learning to hold a conversation is an extremely complex task involving all aspects of language knowledge. This requires skills of attending, listening, processing, comprehending, formulating ideas, formulating sounds to respond, and then listening all over again. These skills then need to be applied to different individuals in different settings.

A child with an autism spectrum disorder also requires modifications to the physical environment to allow him or her to make sense of their world. Parents and caregivers benefit from understanding that autism spectrum disorders often affects the child's physiology. Often, he or she does not deliberately choose to misbehave, tantrum, or make inappropriate statements to others. These children are often responding to the physical and social environment with impairments to their communication and social skills and sensory systems.

Parents and caregivers benefit from taking the perspective of the child with an autism spectrum disorder. From this vantage point, individuals can work to modify the external world of a child to meet his or her needs. For example, since children with autism spectrum disorders have difficulty with transitions from one activity to the next, the use of schedules is often needed. Schedules provide important clues for children with autism spectrum disorders to understand their day.

Such a proactive and accommodating approach is similar to adapting public buildings for persons with visual impairments, deafness, or other physical challenges. Children with autism spectrum disorders can benefit by having accommodations made to their environment. These accommodations facilitate access to services and activities enjoyed by children without autism spectrum disorders.

Thinking from the perspective of a person with autism will help the reader understand the recommendations in this book. An autistic perspective includes the knowledge that children with autism spectrum disorders do not understand social cues, such as how to communicate "Goodbye" appropriately. Children with autism spectrum disorders often have a poor understanding of social situations, like how to play with others.

Sometimes children with autism spectrum disorders elicit strong negative responses from other children, such as ignoring. An example of this is one child ignoring a child with an autism spectrum disorder trying to make small talk.

Children with autism spectrum disorders often feel that their senses are under assault. Pervasive anxiety is common among these children. Frequently, expressive and receptive language problems prevent these children from understanding typical speech.

This book is about making reasonable simple changes to routines, expectations, and environments in order to help children feel more comfortable. Helping a child with an autism spectrum disorder feel safe and comfortable will allow him or her to live better. With proper interventions and accommodations, children with autism spectrum disorders will more effectively relate to others and enjoy life better.

How to use this book

Each topic area includes a story about an experience with a child with an autism spectrum disorder. As in life, experiences in these stories are sometimes very positive and at times, very difficult. There is an analysis of the situation after each of these stories under the heading "What happened?" For example, a visit to a shoe store is explained in terms of the reasons why the child with an autism spectrum disorder had a hard time. "Hints and tips" are then given to help parents and caregivers find solutions to everyday problems in the home and community. Successful approaches to handling these situations come from the authors and from parents and caregivers. Recommendations are given with the specific needs of children with autism spectrum disorders in mind.

1: Home Life

Parents and caregivers know that home life is not typical when you have a child with an autism spectrum disorder. What is taken for granted for most individuals, is often difficult for these children – it is not that these children are trying to act badly or that they do not care about what they do.

The disorder prevents a child from understanding and remembering what we consider simple routines. For example, even going from TV watching to dinnertime can be difficult. It is easy for parents and caregivers to become frustrated. Often this frustration is borne out of the belief that the child "should" be following directions better or that the child is willfully disobeying. Children with autism spectrum disorders are not perfect and can be disobedient just like all other children. Moreover, it is typically not an issue of having the intelligence to do what they are asked. Sensory system, language processing, and other physical issues prevent such children from fitting in easily within the routines of the home and community.

Individuals with typical nervous systems follow signals provided by the environment that children with autism spectrum disorders often do not see or understand. For example, when a parent or caregiver is working in the kitchen to prepare a meal, typically a child will know that the signal will soon be coming that dinner is ready. During this time, the child will prepare him or herself internally for the transition from playtime to dinner. They know they need to wait and to begin to have closure on their play. When the call to dinner that the child has anticipated finally comes, he or she is ready for this transition. Many children with autism spectrum disorders are not able to detect nonverbal environmental signals which indicate a change. For example, they may not associate working in the kitchen with a meal soon to come or getting themselves ready for dinner.

While this chapter does not include every possible difficulty that may be experienced in the home, it does list the most frequently experienced problems as reported by parents. The importance of structuring a child's surroundings is the key to their success in any situation. While rewards and discipline can be used with typical children with a great deal of success, for children with autism spectrum disorders these methods fall short. This is because children with autism spectrum disorders are often responding to internal and external stimuli that are quite overwhelming for them. Again, it is not that they are willfully trying not to follow what they are supposed to do. It is that their surroundings overwhelm them. This is why often the best thing that parents and caregivers can do is to make accommodations to a child's environment.

Babysitters

I was terrified when I first received a telephone call from Mrs. Wilson, Brad's mother, asking me to babysit. I knew Brad and I knew he had autism. I felt a little guilty for being afraid, but I knew very little about autism and I knew even less about Brad. I remembered having seen something on television about autism. In the babysitting course I completed they talked a little about children with special needs. However, that was the extent of my knowledge. I knew who Brad was because we live in a small community and I had seen him around town.

Actually, the last time I saw Brad he was with his father in the grocery store. Brad was having a full-blown temper tantrum because he was not getting a toy that he wanted. He was on the floor screaming in a high pitch sound, crying, and banging his head against his father's legs. I can remember thinking at that time that I did not have the slightest idea of what I would do to handle a child with that kind of a behavior problem.

When Mrs. Wilson called, I knew that she needed a babysitter, because all parents do. I also thought that maybe she needed a babysitter more than most parents because of the demands of having a child with special needs. I asked Mrs. Wilson to tell me about Brad and how she thought I could help.

Brad's autism affected his daily living and I wondered what that might mean for me as his babysitter. She said that Brad didn't speak very much. For this reason, she would give me a schedule and list of things he would need. I felt good about this. She made it sound very simple. I read a little bit about autism, but I found it a little confusing because most of the kids that I was reading about didn't exactly sound like Brad. These children sounded like they were in their own world most of the time and that they would probably need very specialized care. It was hard for me to see how these children could be left with a sixteen-year-old babysitter.

The evening of our first sitting arrived. We agreed that it would be a short evening, not lasting more than two hours. I arrived early to be sure that I had plenty of time to go over Brad's schedule. I wanted to be sure that I understood what I was supposed to do and where I would find what I needed.

The schedule said that Brad would begin the evening with some playtime and then dinner. He would have French fries, a hamburger, and a soda for dinner. I made the French fries and hamburger, but decided to give him water instead of a soda because I was a little afraid that too much sugar in the evening might cause him to become overactive. Everything was fine until I gave him water to drink. Brad flipped out. He shoved the plate of food across the table and screeched. I asked what the matter was, but that only made him get louder. What was wrong? I couldn't figure it out.

I thought that I was doing everything correctly. I had flashbacks of Brad's behavior in the grocery store with his dad. I thought to myself that if Brad's dad couldn't prevent him from having a total meltdown how could I? I called Brad's mom on her cell phone and she said to give Brad soda that was in the refrigerator. I gave him the soda. Brad initially struggled to calm down. He was teary eyed and sighed. I gave him his plate back, and the rest of dinner went fairly well.

Sherry, Brad's babysitter

What happened?

Mrs. Wilson, Brad's mom, did a good job by providing a schedule for the babysitter to follow. She has learned from her own experiences that Brad is a child who requires a great deal of predictability and structure in his life, particularly when there is a major change in routine, as in the case of a new babysitter. Mrs. Wilson and the babysitter, Sherry, were also wise in planning a short two-hour initial session to enhance the likelihood of a successful experience.

It was a good idea that the babysitter came early to get acclimated to the schedule and supplies in the home. However, the babysitter did not understand the reasons that Brad required such a strict regimen. This kept her from understanding that it was in the best interest of the child that she follow the schedule provided to her.

She thought that the evening was going well and that a minor change in the menu would be for the better. After all, Brad is a handsome, "normal" looking kid. At some level, the babysitter most likely thought that schedule was just a guideline rather than an agreement that the child was following and depending upon for predictability. However, the babysitter did not understand the nature of the disability, and, as a result, did not think that she needed to follow such a strict regimen. The babysitter may have even thought that the mother was overprotective when she handed her the schedule.

Hints and tips

Mrs. Wilson knew that in the past she had experienced the benefit of using schedules with Brad. She understood the underlying benefit to her son after having observed him for many years. She discovered that the missing piece in this scenario was that she needed to take more time training Sherry in understanding the underlying deficits that required the use of schedules with Brad.

The babysitter needed to understand that the schedule was a tool used with Brad that provided him with information about events as they unfold. At this same time, the schedule creates a predictable environment. Increased understanding and predictability reduces stress and leads to better self-regulation. The babysitter also needed to know that because of Brad's significant language delays he did not always know what was going on and could not always predict what was going to happen.

Mrs. Wilson recognized that she needed to describe Brad's disability in greater detail. She especially needed to explain the importance of taking the perspective of an individual with autism. She needed to explain how the disability is in many ways a "hidden" disability. Brad looks like every other child, but thinks and responds differently to his world.

Mrs. Wilson provided a schedule for the babysitter, but did not provide a visual schedule for Brad to view. Such a schedule should be provided for the babysitter. The babysitter can point to each step in the schedule as it comes up. Again, children with autism spectrum disorders need such predictability to help them regulate themselves.

Many parents that we talked to suggest that a schedule for a babysitter is used. A sample schedule for a babysitter may look like this:

Choice playtime:

Use choice board with selection of three preferred activities (Chapter 6 has information regarding developing choice boards).

Eat dinner:

Hamburger, French fries and soda with colored straw (of child's choice).

Clean-up:

- Take plate, cup and utensils to the counter.
- Put napkin in wastebasket.
- Use a soft cloth kitchen towel with warm water to wipe child's mouth and hands.

Choice video:

Use choice board with selection of three preferred video programs.

Bedtime routine:

- Get pajamas.
- Dress in pajamas.
- Potty.
- Brush teeth – review micro schedule on mirror.
- Wash face – review micro schedule on mirror.

Choice settle down:

Use choice board with selection of three preferred settling activities.

Choice bedtime:

Read a short book to him of his choice from the book choice board.

Bees

It was a beautiful day in the spring. There were two potted plants outside the front door. Walter was three and a half. I said to Walter, "Let's go outside." We walked out and there were a couple of bees by the bushes.

He flipped his lid, out of his mind, screaming hysterically when he saw the bees. After that day, he is scared to go outside or walk in the grass because of bees, and today, goes inside when he sees a bee. He is now ten. He was never stung by a bee. Somewhere along the line, Walter heard that bees could hurt you. Years later when I went to an Asperger's support group, 95 percent of the parents said their kids were afraid of bees too.

Kris, Walter's mom

What happened?

Children with autism spectrum disorders often think in concrete terms. This is to help them make sense of the world. Walter heard that bees hurt people. He took this to mean that bees always hurt people. Seeing a bee would raise the level of concern in most people. Perhaps they would walk a few steps away. Children with autism spectrum disorders will often have an exaggerated response to such a situation and need assistance in learning how to handle possible dangers.

Hints and tips

While Kris did not have a strategy to help Walter deal with bees, other parents have recommended several activities to help their children get over fears. Presenting a mock scenario ahead of time is an effective way for a child to think about how he or she should act in many situations. Writing down such situations is like having a script in which characters can play out different roles. A child can learn very clear communication patterns in this fashion.

There are many different ways of developing such written scenarios. Behaviorists have used the term "rehearsal" to practice appropriate behaviors before situations arise. "Social Stories"™ (Gray 2000) is a phrase in which a specific formula is used to develop stories in teaching children with autism spectrum disorders. Additionally, the use of the term "script" is often used for individuals with visual impairments to teach them how to navigate in their environment. Here is sample of a written scenario, what we will call a "script," regarding bees that may be used for a child with an autism spectrum disorder:

Day 1
We are going to look out the window today at the flowers. You know, insects and bees cannot get into the house when the doors and windows are closed, so we will be safe looking at insects and bees and flowers through the windows. I put a pretend bee made out of paper on top of one of the bushes and I'd like to see if you see it.

Day 2
We are going to walk outside today and see the make-pretend bee that we found yesterday. We are going to go up to the make-pretend bee and then walk about ten steps away. Let's practice walking ten steps away. This is what you will do when you see a real bee; walk ten steps away. Bees will not bother you when you are away from them. Ten steps are much more than you need to walk, but just in case you are scared, you should walk those ten steps.

The script is practiced several times, until the child knows what to do when he sees a bee. Chapter 6 has additional information about developing scripts.

Breastfeeding

I dreamt of having a baby for as long as I can remember. When I became pregnant with Jonathan, I was so excited. I couldn't believe what a blessing he was and how awesome it would feel being his mother. I had decided years earlier that if I was fortunate enough to have a child, that I would want to breastfeed my baby. While in the hospital, on my first attempt to nurse, I noticed that Jonathan appeared interested and hungry, but he didn't seem to be able to breastfeed. Our attending nurse said not to worry, that this was not uncommon, and that we could try again later in the day. We tried several times with the same results.

With each attempt, the baby was getting more hungry and irritable. I was becoming more frustrated and disappointed. Maybe I couldn't nurse my baby. I felt like such a failure. I decided with the advice of my mother to go ahead and bottle-feed Jonathan so that I would be sure that he would receive adequate nutrition. I discovered two years later that Jonathan had developmental disabilities that negatively affected his speech and language, social, and motor development.

Kim, Jonathan's mom

What happened?

Most developmental disabilities are present at birth. In Jonathan's case, his developmental difficulties first manifested themselves in a weak suckle that was evident to his mother when she was trying to breastfeed him just hours after his delivery. While he was very interested in the breast and was hungry, he was not able to coordinate his oral fine-motor musculature well enough to nurse.

Hints and tips

Kim learned later after her child was born that many children with disabilities are breastfed by their mothers. She learned that experts in the fields of infants with disabilities and nutrition say that it takes patience to do so. Breastfeeding procedures are many times different than for infants without disabilities. The mother needs to hold and train the infant breastfeeding while their oral musculature is maturing. Another option is called a supplemental feeding system. This usually involves an apparatus that is attached to the mother's breast. It allows a baby to feed from the breast and also receive supplemental infant formula. It is recommended that a mother seeks guidance from her physician regarding the use of these specialized techniques.

Kim was disappointed that she had missed her opportunity to nurse her own infant. But she now spends time volunteering and working with an organization that educates medical personnel and parents in the emotional and physical benefits of nursing infants with special needs and in behavioral strategies that make breastfeeding possible.

Dates for parents

My husband and I have not been out together on a date for over six years. It saddens us a bit because we made a commitment when engaged to place our marriage first over all other things. We knew that it would be best for us, our future children, our work and our friendships if we could remain strong as a couple. We have not been able to keep our commitment and now our marriage is strained. Our biggest struggles have been in managing our time, resources, and energy while we parent two beautiful, yet needy children. Hayden is our first child. He is now six years old and Mica is three. Hayden was a very fussy baby who threw-up every time he ate. He didn't just dribble, but he had projectile vomiting that caused a huge mess every time he ate.

He was eventually diagnosed with reflux and was given an appropriate medication that greatly improved the situation. He also has food sensitivities that required a special diet. It was hard having a sick baby and neither of us really wanted to take a chance leaving him in the care of others. We soon discovered that he also has communication difficulties. The specialized diet and therapies that Hayden now required became overwhelming. Just about the time we began to balance our first son's schedule, our second baby was born. Mica was a happy and healthy baby. He did not have the same eating difficulties as his brother, but he had similar communication problems. Both boys are enrolled in speech therapy, occupational therapy, and are on specialized diets. They are making good progress and for that we are thankful. In the meantime we have almost lost our identity as a couple. We want to get back to our original plan and really do not know how or where to begin.

Lauren and Frank, Hayden's parents

What happened?

Lauren and Frank's situation is typical of many parents who want a strong marriage and are challenged by raising a child or children with disabilities. There is often a change of focus away from the stability of the marriage. This change tends to happen over time. Many couples find themselves in the situation of choosing between giving their children everything that they need yet holding back something for themselves and their marriage.

Hints and tips

Parents and couples raising children with disabilities must recognize the importance of caring for themselves and their relationship. It might not make sense to everyone to divert time, energy, and resources to themselves or this relationship. Perhaps an analogy from the airline industry might help to prove a point. When people are traveling by plane, the flight attendants will prepare the passengers for take-off. Passengers will be reminded that in the event of a loss of cabin pressure, oxygen masks will become available. Those adults traveling with young children are advised to put on oxygen masks first, and then provide one for the child. This is, of course, to ensure that the adult does not pass out from a lack of oxygen before being able to care for their child. This same concept can be applied to parenting of children with disabilities. If you do not take care of yourself or your marriage, you could "pass out," and not be able to provide the care that your child requires in the long term.

Suggestions for keeping a marriage and relationship strong include having regularly scheduled dates. Dates are times a couple can spend together for the purpose of sharing intimate conversation and experiences that strengthen the relationship. Couples may need to be creative with their understanding of dating. It is common to think that a date must occur in the evening over dinner at a restaurant. An evening date might not be possible. The time may need to be altered from evening to daytime. Many think that dates must involve some cost. This is also something that can be modified. A date can be a walk through town or on a country road, visiting a local park, or touring a museum with minimal cost. A date can involve a picnic lunch or just a snack from home. If time is a factor, a date can be modified to thirty minutes rather than three hours. Dates that involve some type of exercise have the added benefit of providing stress reduction.

Childcare for dates can come from an exchange agreement with another parent or couple who may also have a child with a disability. The date can happen while the child is in school or attending activities or therapies. Dates that are short in duration, yet frequent, can provide a source of important emotional sustenance to couples.

Discipline

Sometimes I think that the hardest part of having a child with special needs is dealing with all of the advice that others want to give. This has been especially true for Hank and me in the area of Troy's behaviors. Since Troy was eighteen months of age, we knew that something was wrong and that he was developing differently. He didn't begin using single words to express himself until he was three and a half years of age and didn't use sentences until he was five years of age. He also never crawled or walked. He progressed from creeping to running. He pulled himself on his belly and one day he pulled himself up, wobbled around for a few days, and then began to run.

Well, his running was really like an uncontrolled falling forward without actually falling. As he got older, he began running with his arms held out to his side like an airplane, or maybe I should say like a bird. He ran with his arms extended with his hands flapping up and down. It really didn't matter where we were or what we were doing.

Troy would run and flap. He was very agile and never bumped into people or things, but other people were always afraid that he would because he appeared so out of control. Much of the time, Troy made a singing sound while running. That was a signal to us that the running and flapping were pleasurable to him. We learned to live with the running and flapping, because he is such a pleasant kid.

The problem was that others around us, including our parents, family members, neighbors, friends, parents of other children, and total strangers, were annoyed by Troy's unusual behaviors. They frequently had advice for us on how to control our son.

Eventually, we stopped going out of our home, seeing our family, and seeing our friends because we did not want to deal with the constant barrage from well-meaning people telling us how to control our child. In most instances, we had already tried all of the methods that they suggested. We stopped going anywhere. Our family became very isolated.

Julie and Hank, Troy's parents

What happened?

While it was hurtful to be on the receiving end of a barrage of well-wishing advice-giving individuals, it was more harmful for this family to become isolated. Others observed the child's unusual behavior and were interpreting it as a lack of parental guidance. They wanted to help and possibly even "rescue" the family by providing advice. Unfortunately, this caused the family to become withdrawn from others.

Children with autism spectrum disorders are difficult for others to understand. A lack of knowledge and understanding can create uncertainty, fear, and anxiety. Individuals respond to such feelings by withdrawing, becoming overly involved, or even in anger. Families with children with autism spectrum disorders have a unique challenge and that is dealing with these types of feelings in themselves and others.

Hints and tips

After much deliberation, this family realized that they removed themselves from the very people who mattered most in their lives: their family and friends. After thinking about this, Julie and Hank realized that by choosing not to be open in their conversation with family and friends regarding their child, this perhaps made others want to give advice. It could be that the extended family and friends thought that Julie and Hank were oblivious to their child's needs.

Candid conversation could have prevented misunderstandings and promoted a team approach to helping raise the child with special needs. The family decided to call a meeting with friends and their extended family. They shared the child's diagnosis and what that meant in real terms, distributed literature about the disability, and then encouraged family and friends to attend support group meetings with the family in order to learn more about the disability. Attending such groups would allow the extended family and friends to get to know other parents and families in similar circumstances. Hearing information from other families validates the existence of the autism spectrum disorder. It also allows extended family members and friends to become open to understanding information about autism spectrum disorders.

The extended family and friends soon began to get a more appropriate perspective on the child's disability. This in turn allowed them to become a strong support system for this family rather than a source of divisiveness.

Dogs

After we were married, my husband, our dog Lady, and I moved into a two-bedroom flat in the city. It was located conveniently near to our jobs. It is small but is a neat and comfortable place to live. It is also perfectly located for our dog with two pleasant parks located nearby. Lady is a miniature poodle, with curly blond fur, and a lovable demeanor and quiet disposition that is perfect for apartment living.

After three years there, our son Matthew was born. At the age of four, he was diagnosed with autism. Matthew is fascinated to watch Lady as she moves around the flat. Sometimes he will handle her roughly while attempting to touch her. I know that he is not being malicious towards Lady, but he tends to push or poke her sharply on her side to interact with her. Lady is usually very tolerant of these intrusions but she has growled at him on several occasions. Lady is not a young dog anymore and I am very concerned that Matthew may accidentally injure her or that Lady may resort to biting in self-defense.

Margaret, Matthew's mom

What happened?

It appears from Margaret's comments that Matthew finds some sensory pleasure watching Lady's movements. He has not learned how to interact with the pet in an appropriate manner. Children with autism spectrum disorders frequently have sensory systems that are either over or under-sensitive and they may resort to unusual behaviors to stimulate the sensory system. Getting the dog to move by pushing or shoving her could be dangerous and could provoke a bite.

Hints and tips

It is common for a family to have a pet and it is nice when all of the family members can enjoy the pet. Children with autism spectrum disorders may struggle to learn the perimeters for having and caring for a pet. In Margaret's case, there is a two-part solution to this dilemma that has proven to be quite helpful for several parents.

The first step is to use a script to teach the youngster the clear boundaries for pet treatment and care. Matthew could be taught through a script that the dog may be petted on the top of the head and rubbed gently on the back, but may not ever be pushed or shoved. The script may read like this:

> Many families have pets. My family has a pet. We have a dog named Lady. I like to see Lady run. Sometimes I push her to get her to run. This can make Lady mad and she might bite me. I can pet Lady gently on the top of her head or on her back, but I cannot push or shove her. I will watch her run during our boy and dog playtime.

The script should be read each day at a time that is convenient and not at a time when there was a problem with the dog. If the child is a nonreader, the story may be accompanied by photographs, icons, or drawings. More information about developing scripts can be found in Chapter 6.

The second step would be to schedule a couple of "doggy playtimes" during the day so that Matthew knows that he will have an opportunity to engage in one of his favorite activities, but at a time that is good for the dog. During this time, an adult could provide supervision so that Matthew is not pushing the dog and could allow Matthew to give the dog treats for running. This would allow the dog to get exercise and play at the same time Matthew is enjoying his special activity and learning to train a dog. A timer can be used to structure the play session.

Finances

We had many concerns about Kelly's development when he was a toddler. He was our first child. We knew that most children were talking at least in single words by age three, but Kelly was only making vowel sounds and cried rather than making a request for something he wanted. At his three-year well-child check-up, my wife convinced the pediatrician that there might be a problem and she referred us to a child development clinic in a large city near our home. The purpose of the referral was to have Kelly evaluated by a trans-disciplinary team of professionals who were all experts in childhood developmental disabilities.

I called the clinic the day after our physician made the recommendation to schedule an appointment. The clinic staff receptionist was friendly and very helpful. I knew that the evaluation was necessary, but in the back of my mind, I was very concerned about the cost. I knew that the evaluation was going to be very expensive. To my relief I discovered that my medical insurance would cover the majority of the cost of the evaluation. This was good because even our portion of the cost of the evaluation was huge for us.

We were told to arrive early on the day of the evaluation. It was a good thing that we did because we had to park in a garage and walk a very long way to the clinic. The cost of parking was our first insight into the financial aspect of having a child with possible special needs.

The evaluation was very interesting; four child specialists were in the room with my wife and I observing Kelly. One woman, a developmental specialist, introduced toys while trying to engage him in conversation. The others took notes feverishly. Every now and then, the doctor or the speech therapist would make a suggestion to the person working with Kelly to do this or try that. At the end of the evaluation, we met with three of the team members. The results of the evaluation revealed that our son was delayed developmentally so significantly that it would be considered a disability. The name for his disability was autism. We could not believe what we were hearing.

We thought that autism was a rare condition. We had never known anyone with this disability. We had seen it portrayed in TV shows, but in every case, the person was so disabled that they could hardly function without constant supervision. This was not the case for our son. While he was delayed in his development, we could easily see that he would be a somewhat independent person later in life.

At the close of the meeting with the team, each team member took his or her turn explaining to us the types of early intervention Kelly would require if he were to have any chance of reaching his highest potential. It was recommended that he be referred to an early intervention preschool that would include sessions with a speech therapist, occupational therapist, and behavior specialist. They recommended that we begin to attend parent support groups. They also recommended that we investigate community mental health and mental retardation services resources for an in-home behavior support program.

They recommended either therapeutic horseback riding or swimming to help strengthen Kelly's muscle tone. They also talked about using schedules to make the day more predictable for Kelly in order to reduce his frustration. Finally, they recommended a highly structured specialized speech program that would involve our going to another state for intensive training. We were overwhelmed. We struggled to hear everything they were saying enough to even hope that we could implement the recommendations. Lastly, as the manager of the family finances, I was numb. I wanted what was best for my son, but how would or could we possibly pay for all of these services?

Gerrit, Kelly's dad

What happened?

Gerrit experienced what many, if not all, parents experience when faced with the unexpected identification of a child with special needs: the reality of the high financial cost involved in the diagnosing of and treating children with disabilities. It turns out that the cost of the initial evaluation was almost entirely covered by the family medical insurance. But this was just the beginning of the costs related to Kelly's treatment. The number of highly specialized interventions would add up to a large amount of money. Gerrit became anxious about the cost. He was somewhat reluctant to seek many of the therapies recommended without knowing the exact cost involved and how he would be able to pay for such therapies.

Hints and tips

Gerrit carefully read the recommended treatments when his son's written evaluation report arrived in the mail. He listed them in order of priority. The most important recommendation was to get Kelly enrolled in a specialized preschool where he would be evaluated to possibly receive speech and occupational therapy. Knowing that Kelly would need specialized support at school and home, Gerrit asked that home folders be prepared by the school therapists and preschool teacher so that the family could follow through on recommendations at home.

Gerrit then scheduled meetings throughout the year with the therapists. In this way he and his wife could be trained to implement specialized interventions at home and in the community. Gerrit then carefully investigated community services that might provide therapeutic horseback riding and therapeutic swimming lessons. Gerrit and his wife decided that horseback riding lessons would fit within their budget. The stable is located closer to their home and this decreased the cost of transportation.

The family also supported the therapeutic riding stable by starting a fundraising program. Funds were then used by parents who also sought therapeutic riding for their child. The fundraiser involved selling food items that were popular in their area. These items were sold to family, friends, neighbors, and co-workers. The fundraising group also provided the family with a supportive network of other parents who also had children with disabilities.

This group replaced the support group for the family. These families set up respite opportunities for each other that proved to be a valuable resource for many years.

Food

I remember my mother-in-law shoving a piece of hotdog in Kevin's mouth because he refused to eat it. The hotdog was warm, not hot really, but I knew that Kevin was sensitive to spices and hot and very cold foods. Kevin cried of course, and I was upset with my mother-in-law. She's from the old school and doesn't think there is anything wrong with Kevin. She thinks he just has some peculiarities. This is good in a way because I don't want her to think that Kevin has any problems. On the other hand, he is diagnosed with pervasive developmental disorder and she needs to deal with that.

My mother-in-law is not the warmest person on the planet, but she cares deeply for her children and grandchildren. I would like to find a way for her to understand Kevin's disability. I am a little afraid that once she understands what PDD is, she will reject Kevin as being somehow less of a person. However, I do think I have to get over this fear, as she didn't seem to care when we said Kevin was diagnosed. It wasn't that she didn't believe it, it was more as if she thought that the diagnosis was ridiculous. Perhaps there were individuals in her day that were considered "odd" or different and that was that.

Lisa, Kevin's mom

What happened?

There are two issues shown in this story. One issue is the mother-in-law's difficulty accepting the need to recognize the legitimacy of Kevin's diagnosis and her willingness to accommodate for it. The other is the issue of Kevin's sensitivities regarding food.

Concerning food sensitivities, children with autism spectrum disorders are often sensitive to the environment (e.g., air temperature, texture, taste, food temperatures, and food textures). Additionally, children with autism spectrum disorders, like all children, often take a liking to certain foods. For example, a child may want to eat primarily foods with starches like spaghetti and bread.

Hints and tips

Lisa attempts to ensure a balanced diet for Kevin. Many parents say that creativity must be used to make sure that children with autism spectrum disorders do not eat from only one food group. This can be done without over-stimulating the child's sensory system. For example, ensuring that foods are not too hot and not too spicy is important for many children with autism spectrum disorders. Slowly introducing new foods into a diet ensures that it is balanced and that children receive proper nutrition.

In regard to Lisa's mother-in-law, she needs some help in understanding the disorder and how to make accommodations for it. It is only fairly recently that autism and related disorders have become more widely known. There has been a substantial increase in the number of individuals diagnosed with such a disorder in the last few decades. There is not complete agreement among researchers regarding why this is so. It could be that the increased number of individuals diagnosed is the result of better identification of autism spectrum disorders. On the other hand, it may be that many more individuals are showing related symptoms of having these disorders. In either case, parents recommend explaining fully to family members this sort of information. Sharing books and other kinds of information can be helpful to family members helping to raise children with autism spectrum disorders.

Friendships

Elizabeth will talk to her friend not realizing that her friend isn't listening (in fact her friend puts on her speakerphone and plays video games during conversations). Sometimes her friend will say, "Oh, Elizabeth," in frustration. I know things aren't going well. Elizabeth doesn't get it. Her friends are not that interested in her. They often just tolerate her.

Elizabeth has many talents and can be funny. Her classmates see this and want to be around her. Sometimes they tag along with her, but once they get to know her, her friends lose interest. They get annoyed with how she interacts with them. Usually other kids with disabilities seem to get along with her better. Maybe this is because they don't find her to be unusual. I'd like Elizabeth to learn how to make friends.

Susan, Elizabeth's mom

What happened?

Children with autism spectrum disorders often misread social cues. Sometimes they do not know when they are being made fun of, or when others are just tolerating them. They often struggle with interpreting negative cues given by others, such as sighs, a harsh tone of voice, rolling eyes, and turning. Often they are so desperate for friends that that they will allow themselves to be mistreated. Children with autism spectrum disorders can become victims of bullying.

Hints and tips

Susan realized that Elizabeth needed to develop skills to make and maintain friendships. She discovered that her daughter needed to learn how to interpret social cues and how to respond appropriately. She knew that this would have to come from additional training in social skills. For example, when someone says the child's name in frustration, this may be a cue that they are annoyed with the child. Susan discovered that the new skills would need to be taught directly. Direct instruction can be used to teach specific social skills. Parents suggest that a few specific skills are selected at first. For example, you may want to teach your child how to begin a conversation by saying "Hello."

Role-playing can also be used effectively here as well. Role-playing is a method used in teaching the perspective of other individuals and to learn valuable social skills. Role-playing works well because it helps individuals practice in a safe but somewhat authentic setting. Learning then carries over to real events.

To help your child with friendships, it is often necessary to structure playtimes. Some suggestions include limiting the amount of playtime with the friend and providing a list of activities and choices. The section "Play dates" in Chapter 3 provides more suggestions in helping a child with an autism spectrum disorder develop and maintain friendships. Chapter 6 has detailed information about how to do role-playing regarding friendships and how to provide direct instruction.

Susan discovered that these methods worked. She found that direct instruction combined with role-playing and structured play opportunities allowed Elizabeth to progress in her social development.

Holidays

We don't like to say it, but holidays with Jason are usually stressful. When I grew up, the holidays seemed to be a lot of fun. The entire family got together. Even the adults had fun getting together and seeing everyone. Since Jason was born we have had to modify how we approach the holidays. Jason cried and would not come out of his room. If we were at someone's house, he'd bang his head and bite his arm. Following the visit, he wouldn't eat for days and developed bathroom problems. He was stressed and very unhappy with large family gatherings.

We don't go with him to many places, particularly during the holidays. We feel too guilty to leave him home with a babysitter, even if we could find one. So we all stay home together and have a nice time. Perhaps when Jason is older, he will be able to handle the stress of large gatherings.

Maybe it's our issue and we embarrass too easily. Then again, I don't think that it is right for a child to disrupt a family function. There's probably a middle ground between our extended families accepting Jason's uniqueness and Jason doing a better job behaving.

James and Sally, Jason's parents

What happened?

Holidays are a change in routine for everyone. In many cultures, holidays often include candles, bright lights, bright colors, and special foods. Often, there is a gathering of people who do not see each other often. Jason's need for routine was greatly interrupted during the holidays. The festive settings, new people, and crowds over-stimulated his nervous system. Jason responded to these disruptions by withdrawing to his room. When he was not at home, he would respond by harming himself. In both cases he was demonstrating his high level of stress.

Hints and tips

James and Sally planned on waiting until Jason was older to participate in large gatherings. What other parents have suggested is to have children participate in preparing for the special event, such as in making decorations. Select materials that can be tolerated or even enjoyed by your child. Permit your child to stay on his same diet, even though the rest of the family is having special foods. Prepare family members or guests by calling ahead and explaining the accommodations you need to make. You may need to explain why it is that you cannot stay too long, or why you may bring a small box of familiar toys for your child, for example.

We have known families that have decided not to participate in large family gatherings because family members would not be flexible with such accommodations. Many families choose to get together in smaller, more intimate gatherings. Some decide to stay away altogether. However, in many cases this avoidance of family gatherings lasts for a short period. For families with children with autism spectrum disorders, it is often better to stay involved with the extended family and friends with some accommodating. In this way, children with autism spectrum disorders learn from an early age how to handle such holidays and special events.

Marriage issues

After seventeen years of marriage, we were on the verge of a divorce. It was as if we didn't even know each other anymore, we felt like strangers. My husband Jake went to work everyday as an engineer for a large food processing plant and I stayed home in our nice little home providing full-time care for our children, volunteering at school and in the community, and helping to care for Jake's mom when I could. Jake would get home for dinner around 5:00. He would eat and then retreat to the computer or television in the den. I don't remember exactly when we began to drift apart, but I know that it became most evident when our third child Max was diagnosed with autism. We were always stressed by his many needs and difficult temperament. The diagnosis just made us all the more unhappy.

It seemed to me that all of a sudden I became consumed with helping Max overcome his disability. With that, Jake drew farther and farther away. Over the past ten years, I have spent hundreds of hours reading books, attending classes, attending conferences, visiting doctors, visiting clinics, and attending parent support meetings. Now I actually lead workshops for parents and speak at conferences on the topic of autism. Jake has shown very little interest in studying autism although I know that he does care about Max and is glad that I have worked so hard to help him.

Now we come and go with nothing to say. We have little in common, except the children of course, and our time together is not very intimate. We are fighting more frequently and there is very little joy in our relationship. I do not believe that this could possibly be good for the children and it is definitely not good for Jake or myself.

Bailey, Max's mom

What happened?

Bailey was very interested in developing a clear understanding of her son's autism and finding an appropriate treatment. She began to develop a strong personal interest in this topic that began taking a lot of her time. In addition to being a topic of intellectual interest, it was also one of emotional interest. She believed that her son's wellbeing and his future depended upon her research and study. In addition to her internal motivation to pursue this topic, Bailey also received quite a bit of attention from others for her willingness to study hard and to share her personal experiences as the mother of a child with autism.

At some level, she neglected to include her husband in her activities. The new pursuit also took a great deal of her time away from her husband. This caused some animosity between her and her husband, and the siblings and their brother. Overall, this mother ended up with problems that she had not envisioned when embarking on this journey. She was caught between the real need to understand Max's disability and remain committed as a mother and wife.

Hints and tips

Bailey didn't want the seventeen-year marriage to end, yet at the same time she did not want it to continue in its dismal condition. After much thought, she realized that she had taken a new course and neglected to include her husband. Somewhere along that path, she became bitter that he had not joined her. However, how could he have joined her when she did not even invite him to participate?

Bailey decided to confront the issue head-on. She approached her husband and admitted her mistake. She sincerely asked that he forgive her for her insensitivity when she did not include him in the search for treatments and a cure for their son. She also asked that he forgive her for her angry attitude toward him for his not joining in the journey to discover what Max needed. She attempted to make amends by asking if he would like to join her on this journey.

Much to her surprise, he indicated that he would like to join in this pursuit. They began talking together about the topic of autism, about their son, about the progress made in the area of research, and began conducting speaking engagements together.

While there continue to be highs and lows in their marriage, they now have a point at which they can rally and find purpose together. This has strengthened their friendship and their love for each other.

Mealtimes

Al would always cry at dinner. Whenever I called him for dinner, he would ignore me at first. By the fourth or fifth time that I called him for dinner, he would begin screaming and crying. Eventually, he would come to dinner, whining, crying, and disrupting everyone. Then, at dinner, he couldn't stand it when different foods were close together on the same plate. He'd often refuse to eat. Sometimes he would yell about how the different foods were touching on his plate. Once I asked him to help set the table and he yelled and cried.

It's been exasperating trying to have a normal family dinner with Al. Now, many times, it's easier for him to eat before the rest of the family. A sandwich and some milk seem to make him happy. I am concerned that he is not getting a balanced diet, and really want the family to eat together. I think this would be a good goal for us. We would try anything to make this work.

Mary Kay, Al's mom

What happened?

Kids with autism spectrum disorders need a routine. There are certain things parents and caregivers have to change in the environment to help these kids succeed. Mixing foods is very often a cause for concern for children with autism spectrum disorders. These may be due to the child wanting the familiar. A child may like mashed potatoes and corn.

Children with autism spectrum disorders need the familiar including how food is arranged on a plate. This is because they often have a rigid and concrete view of the world. They like to have aspects of their lives compartmentalized. This results in often not liking different foods mixed together on the same plate.

Additionally, mealtime is a change in a child's schedule. For children with autism spectrum disorders, to switch from playing or watching TV to having to sit down for dinner can be difficult. Another layer of stress is added because mealtimes require socialization with others and a whole host of skills that a child needs to show. Mealtimes are times for talking, using manners, and routines that we take for granted (e.g., first salad, then the main course, and then dessert).

Hints and tips

The use of schedules cannot be overemphasized. A schedule may be used for dinner, or any mealtime. It may look like this:

1. Sit down to dinner.

2. Put napkin on lap.

3. Say "thank you" when you receive your food.

4. Eat your food.

5. Bring your plate to the sink when Mom or Dad says that dinner is done.

Parents indicate that for children with autism spectrum disorders who cannot read, a visual picture schedule may help. Drawings or even photographs in a series can work quite well. For children with visual impairments, a texture or object may be used. An object schedule may include a dining table from a dollhouse or even real food items. In addition, it is important that all family members understand why it is that the child needs a schedule.

A timer may be used to show visually how long dinner will last. Sectional plates, like those used in picnics, may be helpful for keeping foods separate on children's plates. Using the same routine, such as seating individuals in the same place during each mealtime, may be helpful.

Humor is often helpful as well. Some parents I know make a funny face in sandwiches using condiments, such as mustard.

Morning and nighttime routines

I found the true meaning of frustration was having to give the same direction, the same command, the same prompt, in the same way for every task completed 365 days a year for six years. I did this until I discovered the value of the morning and nighttime routines. My daughter Michelle would wake up early every morning and begin to play with her favorite toys. She frequently played with her puzzles or building blocks. I would hear her and I would get up to begin the day's activities. Everyday started the same with my telling her what to do step-by-step. If I missed a step, she would stop and wait for me to get it right. She had become very dependent upon my verbal prompts to tell her what do, when to do it, and how to do it. This was very time-consuming and exhausting for me.

The morning prompts would sound something like this:

"Good morning Michelle. It is time to have breakfast. Come to the kitchen and sit down. Eat your breakfast. When you are finished, please place your dishes in the sink. Now it is time to get dressed. Go to your room and put on the pants and top that are on your dresser. Go to the bathroom to brush your teeth. Now brush your hair. Get your shoes and socks. Sit down and let me put your socks and shoes on your feet. Get your book bag. Get your jacket. Let's watch for the school bus. It is time to go to school. Goodbye, have a great day!"

I could recite this routine in my sleep. We had a very similar routine for bedtime. The only major difference was that Michelle always asked for a review of the next day's schedule before she went to sleep the night before.

In addition to being tired with the verbal routine, I was becoming very concerned that Michelle becoming dependent upon my prompts. She was not developing independent skills for self-care. I thought that it would be virtually impossible for another person to get her ready for school in the morning. It would be hard for someone to help without knowing the verbal script for the morning or bedtime routines.

Sabrina, Michelle's mom

What happened?

Sabrina found that her daughter Michelle was happier and functioned better when she was given short verbal commands when required to complete simple routine functions. Michelle's language delays and need for sameness prompted Sabrina to begin using the short verbal commands for her daughter's morning and nighttime routines. The problem is that Michelle became dependent upon the verbal prompts, rather than becoming independent. The verbal prompting was time consuming for Sabrina and restrictive for Michelle.

Hints and tips

Sabrina discovered that Michelle needed directions for daily living. She needed tasks broken down into small manageable chunks and, at the same time, she needed to be able to have some practice completing tasks independently. After much thought, Sabrina created a morning and nighttime routine using visual schedules that mirrored the verbal schedule that she had used over the years. The verbal schedule worked well, but it had two major drawbacks. It was exhausting for Sabrina and it reduced Michelle's opportunities for doing these skills independently.

Sabrina introduced the visual schedule to Michelle and then rewarded her efforts to use the schedule. She used a candy treat and verbal praise initially. She was also very careful not to talk too much about the schedule, but to use a very simple phrase like "check schedule" when Michelle seemed to be confused. After a couple of weeks, Michelle used the visual schedules independently. Sabrina was pleased with the progress. Michelle seemed to be proud of her ability to function more on her own.

Noise

Dylan held his ears during assemblies in kindergarten. He hated to go to the auditorium because of the noise. Balloons popping would also make him hold his ears. It was about this time that we suspected that Dylan was different. We didn't see other children holding their ears during assemblies. Other children actually appeared to enjoy the loud popping balloons. First grade did it for us however. Dylan's teacher didn't say anything. Nevertheless, between Dylan holding his ears and seeing him lie on the classroom floor (the teacher said he did this often), we thought we should have him evaluated. I remember seeing some news program or something like that where kids flapped their arms, dangling keys in front of their eyes, or holding their ears.

Over the next year, Dylan became interested in big trucks. In fact, a place near our home has tractor pulls and demolition derbies. The first time we went, I was worried because I knew it was going to be loud. I thought though that this might help. Dylan could maybe get over his fear of loud noises.

The sounds at these events were some of the loudest sounds that I ever heard. We both held our ears! Around the second year of going to these events, Dylan said to me, "I don't need to hold my ears anymore." Although we both didn't have to anymore, I got us earplugs to protect our eardrums.

Thunderclaps, the vacuum cleaner, and the lawnmower don't seem to bother Dylan anymore. He still has normal hearing, according to the school nurse. It was as if his body somehow matured.

Jeff, Dylan's dad

What happened?

Dylan is showing what is often typical for children with autism spectrum disorders: sensitivity to noise. Sensory systems can develop over time however. Many parents report improvements in how their children respond to stimuli, such as noise in the environment, over the years. Dylan may have also became less fearful of some loud noises because they were not viewed as a threat any longer.

Hints and tips

Dylan improved because Jeff challenged his son in a supportive manner. Such an approach is the key to helping children with autism spectrum disorders.

Individuals with autism spectrum disorders often have a heightened awareness of sounds and all senses. Sounds feel louder for these children. Children with autism spectrum disorders can be taught compensatory strategies for dealing with loud sounds. Rather than wail and scream in response to a loud sound, a child with an autism spectrum disorder can be taught and then coached to use responses that are more appropriate. For example, they can ask for ear plugs or tell an adult that a sound is too loud or bothersome.

Some parents report that drawing simple pictures of situations and a follow-up picture of how the child should respond is an effective way to teach a child with an autism spectrum disorder how to handle difficult situations. Such pictures can be drawn or written about traffic, lawn mowers, and vacuum cleaners, or any other loud event. It is important that the pictures relate to something important in your child's life. Comic strip conversations are also an effective method for teaching appropriate responses to many different situations (Gray 1994). Essentially, comic strips can be drawn by parents and customized to meet the specific needs of their children to address difficult situations.

Organization

Luke's stuff is everywhere. If someone buys him a toy, like a handheld video game system, parts go missing by the end of the week. He's gotten some expensive stuff that he likes an awful lot. Even Luke gets upset when things are lost. He wants to keep his things. We got him a special case for the video game system, to hold games, manuals, and so on. Even so, things get misplaced. Luke doesn't follow procedures we've set up for him to return items to specific boxes or locations in the house. We have to remind him each time he comes into the house to put away his sneakers. We are kind of at a loss as to how to help Luke keep his things organized. He has Asperger Syndrome, and we think this has something to do with it.

Leah, Luke's mom

What happened?
Children with autism spectrum disorders often have difficulty being organized. Even children without such disorders have trouble putting away their things. Due to sensory system difficulties in children with autism spectrum disorders, self-care, learning, and organization are greater challenges for these individuals.

Hints and tips
Children with autism spectrum disorders need added clues in their environment to help them function better. For instance, schedules are used to structure a child's day. Procedures posted in appropriate places around the house help children with autism spectrum disorders to make sense of the home.

In the scenario above, it was a good idea for Luke's mom to get a special case for his video game system and all of the items that go with it. However, Luke needs more help in functioning independently with this toy. Leah cannot be in the position of monitoring all of Luke's toys and items throughout the house. Luke needs to do this.

To help Luke remember to put things back in the video game system case when he is done playing, the following suggestions may be used. Attach each component of the game system by string to the case. In other words, each game, which is about the size of a matchbook, can have a string attached using tape or glue. The strings need to be long enough so that the items they secure do not interfere with game play.

In regard to Luke's sneakers, parents have suggested a method for keeping children's shoes organized. A photograph with a picture of Luke's sneakers with an arrow printed on it (with marker) can be used to show where the sneakers need to go. Children with autism spectrum disorders often have difficulty with visual-spatial concepts. It could be that Luke gets confused regarding where to put his sneakers. Visual cues can help in this and in a great many other situations to help such children orient effectively to their environment.

Preferences

In the early years, we thought that Derek's interests were a little odd, or maybe even eccentric. When we learned that the strong interests were one of the characteristics that led the developmental specialist to diagnose him with autism, we were horrified. His first noticeable special interest was in cars. He was obsessed with cars. "Car" was one of his first words and he must have said it five hundred times every day.

We didn't think much about it at the time because it seemed that every little boy was obsessed with cars. His next interest was in trains and again this didn't seem so unusual because many children like trains. It wasn't such an unusual topic, but it was the intensity of his interest that about drove us crazy. Trains were all that he wanted to talk about, the only toys he would play with, and the only cartoon video he would watch. The topic of trains consumed every conversation.

We were beginning to notice that Derek's interests were unusual, but it wasn't until he developed an obsession for garbage cans that we began to think that something might really be wrong. He wanted garbage can toys, he regularly gathered all of the garbage cans in the house and stacked and sorted them. He did everything he could to get outside to the large garbage can we kept in the alley. We even caught him on several occasions trying to drag home the neighbors' garbage can from behind their house. It was also about this time that we were having concerns that his language, fine-motor, and social development might be delayed. He was behind other children in his milestone achievements according to the child development checklists in his baby book.

We decided that it was time to have Derek evaluated by a developmental specialist. We never thought that Derek's strong special interests or preferences would be the piece of information that completed the picture for the evaluator to render a diagnosis of autism. When the specialist shared the results of the evaluation, we were not surprised that she found Derek's receptive and expressive language to be delayed. We were not surprised when she found that his social skills were also delayed. When she indicated that his stereotypic and obsessive behaviors related to his strong special interests meant that he met the criteria for an autistic spectrum disorder, we couldn't believe it.

Our first actions after the evaluation were to try to squelch Derek's odd and eccentric behaviors. We tried taking away all of his cars and trains. However, that didn't work. This caused Derek to become very unhappy. He cried and paced around the house. This seemed to cause him to focus even more on the garbage cans. We were also concerned that he might just pick up another special interest. Maybe that interest would be worse.

We never spoke about how others might view Derek and his autism. We didn't want anyone to know Derek had autism. We also didn't want to accept it ourselves because perhaps this would set him up for failure.

In addition to our concerns about what others might think, we really were concerned that Derek's interests were so strong that they would interfere with him doing other things, like learning, playing with other toys, playing with children, engaging in arts and crafts, or sports. We knew that we had to do something, but what could we do?

Cecelia and Marcus, Derek's parents

What happened?

Cecelia and Marcus were faced with a situation very common to parents of children with autism. The criteria for autism include qualitative impairments in the area of language development, social development, and the presence of stereotypic and repetitive behaviors. These stereotypic and repetitive behaviors frequently present themselves as strong special interests or preferences. In Derek's situation, his interests in cars and trains were typical for his age, the garbage cans were a little unusual. However, it was not the specific items, but rather the strength of his interests in them, that was problematic.

Cecelia and Marcus were struggling with the diagnosis of autism. They also were not exactly sure what the term autism would mean for them and their child. They were fearful that if they embraced the label that they might doom their son to a life with far less potential. They were also fearful that their son would not engage in other types of learning if he stayed preoccupied with his special interest items.

Hints and tips

Cecelia and Marcus soon realized that Derek's interests must fill some
sort of need for him. They learned that Derek's special interests served a
number of purposes in his life. They knew that these interests gave him
pleasure and enjoyment. The special interests also provided predictability because Derek would know what he was going to play with and how
he would play. His special interests calmed him and gave him a connection with other people. Derek showed other people his cars, trains, and
garbage cans. The special interests gave Derek a way to interact with
other people. He used these interests as conversation starters. He
received various types of positive reaction from other people. With this
new found knowledge, Cecelia and Marcus knew that they couldn't take
the items of interest away. So how did they get Derek to be less obsessed
to the exclusion of other learning?

They decided to set up times in the day that Derek was free to engage
in playtime with his toys of special interest. They also decided to employ
the Premack Principle, which indicates that people will be more likely to
agree and participate in less desirable activities, if they know that they
will then be able to engage in a preferred activity afterwards. Cecelia and
Marcus used first-then statement cards (see Chapter 6 for more information) to teach Derek this concept. He would need to do a task such as
cleaning up his room before he could have playtime, for instance. The
required task was listed on one half of the card, and his reward, playtime
with his special interest toy, on the other half of the card. Derek was
shown the card to indicate what he would receive if he completed the
required task. This solution decreased Derek's perseverative behavior
and at the same time increased his involvement in other needed tasks.

Preparing simple meals

> Drew loves to eat and has a great appetite. He has the intelligence to understand different ingredients and can read very well. My husband and I decided that he could begin to fix some of his own meals, like lunch. Drew has problems with his eye–hand coordination. Also, he has low muscle tone in his hands, so cutting and spreading is a problem. Drew has trouble finding things, but with concentration, can do so (especially when it's a video game that he wants to play!). Drew likes hot dogs, so this is how we helped him make his own lunch, which includes a drink, a sandwich, chips, and a treat. We began to write a cookbook for Drew. Each time we want to teach him another cooking skill, we add this to his cookbook binder.
>
> Derrick and Sandy, Drew's parents

What happened?

Drew's parents understand the difficulties that he has in organizing himself and materials in his environment. They also understand that intelligence has nothing to do with Drew being able to prepare his own lunch. Problems with executive function, including remembering directions, are evident in Drew's ability to prepare meals. Supports are needed for children with autism spectrum disorders so that they can learn to be as independent as possible. With practice and maturation, Drew will likely need fewer prompts and written directions to make meals.

Hints and tips

Drew's parents provided the following directions to him in his cookbook regarding making a lunch consisting of hot dogs and other items:

1. Get two plates (above dishwasher).

2. Get hot dogs (from refrigerator).

3. Place one hot dog on one plate.

4. Put plate with hot dog in microwave. Follow hot dog directions on microwave.

5. Get one hot dog roll or one slice of bread (from above microwave) and put it on the plate.

6. When the microwave "beeps," use a fork to put the hot dog on the roll or slice of bread.

7. Get ketchup (from refrigerator) and squeeze it onto the hot dog.

8. Get chips (from above the microwave) and put on the plate.

9. Pour yourself juice (from the refrigerator) or water into a glass.

10. Get a treat (from pantry).

11. Eat your lunch.

12. Put dirty plates and glass in the sink.

13. Put items away.

14. Wash your hands.

It is important that instructing any child includes presenting new materials in small steps. Drew's parents do this by adding a new meal menu only after one has been learned. Frequent review of lessons learned is very important in the teaching process. As such having a binder of previously learned menus is of great assistance to Drew. From time to time, a review of each menu in his binder will help Drew be successful in making meals on his own.

Respite care

Our life is so busy. My husband works very long hours and I work part-time in a home business to make ends meet. We have four children who are of school age and are involved in many after school and community activities. In addition to the daily living requirements such as cooking, cleaning, laundry, and driving our children from one activity to another, our middle son Jamison has special needs.

Jamison was diagnosed at three years of age as having autism. He has delayed language skills, weak gross and fine-motor strength, and behavioral problems. To help Jamison develop his motor and language skills he attends specialized therapies each week. He is currently taking therapeutic swimming lessons once a week and receives private speech therapy twice a week. To address his behavior and social development, along with helping the family cope and work with Jamison, we are all involved with a therapist one evening a week. Taking Jamison to his therapies and spending the time required in follow-up activities recommended by the physical and speech therapists is hard work.

In order to keep track of all our appointments and activities for the entire family, I use a large wall calendar. With this system, our days generally go fairly well, but I am tired. My husband and mother try to help when they can. The therapies are expensive, as are the activities that we offer our other children, so that they don't feel left out. My mom will sometimes come over for an evening to give me a break and I have actually been able to go away overnight once.

In spite of the extra help, I am in a state of chronic fatigue. I can't seem to feel rested, even with an hour extra sleep a night. I am becoming very concerned that I may become ill from the stress. We thought about a vacation away from home and away from all of the activities. However, with Jamison's constant needs and difficulty adapting to new places, this would probably make the experience more stressful than if we just stayed at home.

Rachel and Wade, Jamison's parents

What happened?

Like many families trying to balance the demands of daily living, offering their children opportunities to explore interests, and advance their quality of life, this family is overwhelmed with the stress of a busy schedule. When they learned that their child had extra requirements for care, they also found that their schedule would be very difficult. For this family, days, weeks, and months of uninterrupted activity took its toll including chronic fatigue for the mother. The particular nature of their son's disability made going to new places and changes in the schedule hard to do. Jamison really struggled with adapting to new places, would not be able to sleep, eat, and would become very irritable. This prevented the family from getting away for a vacation.

Hints and tips

Rachel and Wade recognized that they had two problems. The first was that their family was entirely too busy. The second was that the family could not go away on vacation.

The first step was to gather for a family meeting. At the meeting, each person was asked to drop one activity from his or her schedule. They used the wall calendar to list all of their activities. For those children who struggled to give up one activity, other options for being involved in that activity were explored. It was decided the eldest child would drop one sport as a year round activity and just play the sport recreationally in the neighborhood. This was as opposed to her being involved with a sports team. Each child and adult made one choice. The family sought more time with the speech and language therapist at Jamison's school. This replaced the language therapy sessions outside of school.

Lastly, the family decided that they needed a time to get away from the demands of their busy lives. They decided that based on the needs of their family, several short vacations for three or four days each would meet their needs better than one long vacation each year. Even if the family was able to get time away, this still posed a problem because Jamison was not able to adjust to being away from home. The family decided to explore the possibility of respite care for Jamison. This involved a trained person coming to the family home and caring for the child while they went away.

In order to be sure that the respite care would meet Jamison's needs Rachel and Wade searched for the right caregiver. They requested names from agencies that already served children with special needs. They then brought the caregiver to their home on a regular basis to train him and to allow Jamison to become familiar with him. They sought suggestions from the therapist for activities that could enhance the relationship of the caregiver and Jamison. Then they planned a schedule for Jamison and the caregiver that would be enjoyable while the family was away.

Restaurants

We have three children, one of whom has pervasive development disorder. He is our third child. We got used to traveling with our first two children. We went camping, to the beach, and out to eat. We read many books on raising kids and talk to our parents and friends about what is best. Suggestions for good parenting included setting clear rules for expected behavior and consistent follow-through. Rewards are given for good behavior, and punishment for poor behavior. Many of the things we did with our first two kids came in handy with Steven, except that he needed more of the same. For example, he needs to be told way ahead of time, and several times for that matter, before we go anywhere. He also needed rewards more often than our other children. Steven doesn't do as well when he has to wait.

We have been able to travel almost as much as when we just had two kids, and it's not that Steven holds us back, but that three kids is a lot harder than two, with or without a disability. We're proud of ourselves because we expect appropriate behaviors from Steven and we give him supports to help him get there. I see kids in stores and in restaurants who behave much worse than any of our children. Any uniqueness that Steven shows is completely acceptable to us.

Angie, Steven's mom

What happened?
Angie sums up what many parents with children with disabilities believe. Often times with good interventions and a proactive approach to teaching a child social skills, a child can behave as well or better than children without disabilities. All children benefit from being taught directly such skills, such as what to do at a restaurant. In fact, even adults read books on etiquette to learn social skills themselves.

Hints and tips
In Steven's situation, Angie discovered that he needed direct instruction in social etiquette, more time to prepare himself for family outings, and less time between receiving rewards after exhibiting certain desirable

behaviors. Children with autism spectrum disorders need a lot of pre-viewing before trips out of the house. Good table manners start at home. Children with autism spectrum disorders also need to be reminded that manners learned at home need to be displayed in other places. High expectations are important for such children. Biting, kicking, screaming, etc., are not acceptable. What you believe your child can achieve, he or she can, with the right interventions. It may take time and lots of work, but good attitudes from parents and caregivers are essential to the success of the child.

Some parents say that to ready a child for a trip to the restaurant, it is good to practice at home (role-playing). The table is set and someone asks the child what they would like to eat (yes, make up a menu!). Write down what the child would like to eat. Practice a ten-minute wait period before the meal arrives. Allow them to play with their fidgets (small objects the child can manipulate) during this wait time. Practice delivering courses one at a time. Dinner conversation can be worked on. The reward for good behavior is a calm, enjoyable meal.

Some parents tried previewing a sample menu before going to the restaurant. One parent also tried take-out from the restaurant first before taking the whole family there. This way they were able to tell if everyone would like the food. Sitting in the non-smoking section helps. Some parents bring the child's favorite cup. They also suggest that you sit by a window so that your child may watch cars and trucks go by.

In summary, it is helpful to let your child know of the outing well ahead of time. Place the activity on the schedule that he or she may use. Finally, decrease the time between a desirable behavior and the reward given.

Siblings and other relatives

My brother Sam has Asperger's. I feel sorry for him. However, I'm getting used to him flapping. When he was with our grandparents for a month, I missed his flapping. When I'm around him, sometimes we have problems. Sometimes I fight with him and the bad thing is he bites me and kicks me with his feet. To me, I think that is dangerous. My brother gives me ideas. He's smart. When I want to pick a video game at the electronics store, he gives me ideas of what to pick and what not to pick. He likes to go on the computer a lot and find out cheats for games online. The way he makes friends is by making up jokes. At dinner, sometimes he flaps and that makes everyone stop eating. He is a good kid.

Peter, Sam's brother

What happened?

Peter has ambivalent feelings about his brother that are typical of any sibling relationship. The feeling may be a bit stronger due to his brother Sam's atypical behaviors. Sam has some unique differences that make understanding of the syndrome difficult at times. Peter says that Sam can be disruptive, like at dinner. Peter is able to see very positive characteristics of Sam, such as playing games together. Peter clearly loves his brother, and perhaps like all siblings, can feel frustrated at times. It is very positive that Peter can talk about his experiences.

Hints and tips

Siblings of children with autism spectrum disorders need parents who can honestly explain the positive and negative aspects of the disability. Parents find success when they talk about the "label." It helps when parents and siblings know that a disability is only one part of an individual's personality and physical makeup. Brothers and sisters need to know that siblings with disabilities can find joy and happiness in the world.

Siblings need to be able to talk about their experiences with a brother or sister who has an autism spectrum disorder. In fact, many parents tell us that they ask their children pointed questions about this. For example, one parent asked how their son feels about the brother who gets special food and gets to sit on the "comfortable" sofa all the time.

Siblings are often afraid to talk about their feelings because they might not feel that it is okay to "complain" about a brother or sister with a disability. Parents say that it is helpful to tell their children that it is acceptable to be honest about even very negative feelings towards their brother or sister. Parents also say that they let their children vent to them and then also talk about positive aspects of having a sibling with a disability. Many parents also suggest that specifics about a disability be discussed. Be truthful about how stressful it can be on the family to have a child with an autism spectrum disorder. However, it is critical that families have a positive attitude about the situation. A child with an autism spectrum disorder is a person first.

Support groups

Melinda was enrolled in preschool when she was three years old. She struggled to get along with other children. By the time she was five years old, she had already been expelled from two preschools. This was humiliating and at the same time of tremendous concern for us. Her third preschool referred us to a local pediatric clinic that evaluated her and diagnosed her with Asperger Syndrome. We already knew a little bit about the disorder because we had been searching online constantly for any information about her symptoms. We looked for information about her ritualistic behaviors and poor social skills.

The clinic staff recommended that we get involved in several of their programs. The program that I found to be most helpful was the support group. The group met once a week. We talked about our children and how autism was affecting our lives. The structure of the group was one of support and sharing. We were not to share advice with the other parents, but if someone heard something that they liked during a meeting, staff members were always available after the meeting to answer questions. I attended these meetings regularly.

During this time, I made many friends with other parents of children with autistic spectrum disorders. Those friendships led us to getting together outside of the clinic for meals and even larger family gatherings. This was a marvelous time, but it ended when my husband was transferred to a job in the countryside. Before he agreed to the new work assignment, we talked about the benefits and disadvantages at length.

I knew that the biggest loss for me would be the system of support that we had over the years. However, the transfer meant a promotion and a large pay increase. I decided that if a parent and caregiver support group did not already exist, I would start one in our new community. Melinda was becoming a preteen. I knew that I would need help guiding her through these years, especially with her social problems. I just knew that there would be other families with children with Asperger Syndrome. We would just have to find each other.

After moving and being settled in our new home, I began looking for a parent support group. I asked my physician, called several therapists in the telephone book, and contacted the local hospital. I learned that there were no groups in existence there. When school started, I asked my daughter's special education teacher if he knew of any group that was already meeting. He did not know of any group. I started a group, which turned out to be very successful.

Amanda, Melinda's mom

What happened?

Amanda, like many parents, found support from others who were also raising a child with special needs. She and her husband were able to make friends from the group that expanded to include the entire family. When they moved, Amanda and her husband wanted to continue to be involved in a support group in their new community.

Hints and tips

After contacting every resource that she could think of, Amanda started her own group. She started by asking one other mother from Melinda's class to come over for coffee. The other mother agreed, and they began getting together once a week for an hour of coffee and sharing. Each of them invited another parent and before long, there were five parents meeting on a regular basis to provide support for each other. From this group a parent network was started that resulted in large group family get-togethers. This support system provided valuable help to Amanda and Melinda throughout Melinda's teen years. It even provided Melinda with several friends who also had autistic spectrum disorders.

Talking about disabilities

Hello, this is from me, Franklin. I am eleven years old and more mature than a normal Asperger Syndrome kid. I am currently in sixth grade. My favorite sport is flapping (I'm kidding!). I love video games, unique graphics, sound, and picture quality, and high-speed, multiplayer games. My favorite food is hamburgers. I really like it when people understand my needs and desires. Anyways, I want everyone to know how to help Aspergery kids. And how to make excuses up for less work from school (ha!). And now I really want to tell you about all the people who have been helping me out, even though you might not know them. Mom, Dad, my brother Nick, my grandparents, and many more people.

When doing sports like basketball and baseball, I pretty much suck at it. I also suck at riding a bike and having balance. I don't like cabbage, cheese, or chocolate ice cream. I like hamburgers, chocolate, sauerkraut, caramel, butter popcorn, and mostly anything with sugar.

My favorite place to go outside the house is inside (ha!). I do pretty well with making friends and just recently, I learned that I'm popular. Someone told me.

What is hardest for me in my life is homework. It depends on which homework. Like in math, it goes quick. Studying for tests is hard.

I like that I have two cute sisters. I also like that my oldest brother Nick is around. Otherwise, I would be afraid to go in the pool alone when there are only adults when I am at my grandparents' house. I like that I can trick my youngest brother Matt into everything.

I love my mom because she is the most understanding person of all. I also like Mom because she gets me out of trouble like when I spit and when Dad won't be fair. I like Dad because if he wasn't there, who would get me new video games?

My grandparents are great because they buy me anything I want and I talk on the phone constantly with them. Also, they give me a break from all the hard work of school and the family. They also let me go out to eat every night when I visit. I go to sleep well because before I sleep I have a nice hour of flapping and looking at magazines.

I saw one movie in three years due to my being afraid of being freaked out by the sounds in the theater. I could go on and on about myself, but I know you have other things to do.

Franklin

What happened?

Franklin lives in a family that is open about his disability. His strengths are reinforced. Asperger Syndrome is just one piece of his life. For example, Franklin's ability in reading and his good relationships with his parents, siblings, and peers are stressed. While there is discussion about the term "Asperger Syndrome", Franklin's symptoms are discussed. Franklin's parents work with him, his teachers, and siblings on how to help him adapt to his surroundings. Additionally, Franklin is expected to help his siblings. For example, his job is to get his sisters' coats when going outside in the winter. This helps to build Franklin's self-confidence.

Franklin has begun to accept having Asperger Syndrome. For example, he is able to have a sense of humor about his flapping. On the other hand, it bothers him when his brother calls him "Asperger Kid" or sometimes "Ass-perger Kid" when he is mad at Franklin. Overall, Franklin's account shows a family that communicates well and concentrates on strengths.

Hints and tips

Parents suggest what Franklin's parents have done. They suggest being open and honest about problems, but focus on the positives. Franklin's Asperger Syndrome is dealt with in truth and reality. It is not the best situation and not the worst either. Other parents suggest that families watch videos together or read books about family members with autism spectrum disorders. They also suggest going to autism spectrum disorder support groups and setting up play dates with other children with autism spectrum disorders. Children with autism spectrum disorders sometimes want to play with other children with similar disabilities.

It is important that no matter the methods or materials used to talk about autism spectrum disorders with family members, an open and honest forum is available to discuss thoughts and feelings. Children will tend to bottle up such feelings unless they are encouraged to discuss them with a receptive adult.

A child with a disability often wants to know what his disability is and what it is not. Parents often say that they explain to their child that the disability is not the whole person. Children with disabilities are people first. The disability comes second. Some families attend support groups together. Often these children, and all children for that matter, have a great need to understand themselves and to be accepted by others as well.

Tantrums

Being a parent of Hadden was not fun for the first five years of his life. It was a frustrating experience because he cried all of the time. He cried when he got up in the morning, at playtime, during his bath, during his meals, and at bedtime. No matter what we did, we could not soothe him. He seemed to be troubled by fast movement, bright lights, new people, new places, and changes in his schedule. He appeared to be very sensitive to heat and to cold. He couldn't tolerate being too hot or too cold.

He would begin screaming when he was hot. I would have to rush to get the air conditioner turned on or remove some of his clothing. If he felt too cold, he would get upset and I would have to rush and add some layers of clothing. If I gave him a blanket, it couldn't be just any blanket. It had to be his favorite satin blanket.

I remember watching parents at the park interacting with their kids and I was jealous. They played, laughed, wrestled, shared, and in general, enjoyed each other. It was a marvelous thing to see. I couldn't figure out why I was not able to have this same relationship with my son. I was constantly asking myself what I was doing that was wrong, but I just couldn't identify the problem.

When Hadden was nine months old, we asked our physician to try to help us identify the cause for his distress. His pediatrician diagnosed the problem as colic, but we struggled to identify exactly what colic was and how it should be treated. The problem continued and we thought that Hadden might be lactose intolerant. We removed cow milk products from his diet. When he was eighteen months of age, he was evaluated by a gastroenterologist. This person thought that the problem might be acid reflux or irritable bowel syndrome. The gastroenterologist prescribed a specific medication for reflux and said that we should take a wait and see approach. We made a number of dietary changes to address the stomach and bowel issues. All of the treatments seemed to improve the situation for a short time, but then the crying and tantrums would come back.

At about two and a half years of age, we took Hadden to be evaluated by a child psychiatrist. The psychiatrist thought that the crying and irritability were due primarily to issues of temperament. He said that Hadden appeared to be a highly sensitive child, who was struggling to adapt and who was very intense. The doctor told us that this particular combination of temperamental traits made adjusting and changing to circumstances of living very difficult and distressing for our son. The behaviors were exacerbated due to his inability to communicate using words. Hadden communicated his frustration and irritability with behavior in the form of crying and tantrums.

We knew about the concept of temperament, but we didn't think that this could possibly explain the severity of Hadden's problems. He really appeared to us to have physical pain and discomfort.

This whole experience brought about huge feelings of inadequacy in each of us because we could not interpret our child's needs. Was he really hurting and in pain? What made things even worse was that we couldn't comfort him.

Brian and Ivy, Hadden's parents

What happened?

Hadden is a child with a sensitive emotional and nervous system, which was evident in his intense responses to heat, cold, and other situations. He struggles to adapt to change and demonstrates a high need for predictability. The medical treatments that appeared to make a difference for a short period appeared to do so by placebo effect for the parents. When the parents began a new treatment, they became hopeful that Hadden's behaviors would improve. This expectation and the change in their behavior towards Hadden may have helped him to adapt a little better for a few days. However, the crying would eventually return to the same level as in the past.

Hints and tips

Brian and Ivy sought every type of medical intervention before learning that their son's severe agitation and discomfort were more closely linked to his temperament than his physiology. They began to understand that Hadden was a very sensitive baby and that almost every discomfort could be linked to him not being able to regulate his nervous system well. They were then able to enact some effective interventions.

Brian and Ivy began to take a much more structured approach to rearing Hadden. They tried to predict what environments would cause him discomfort. They began planning for those environments. When it was possible to avoid the provoking environment, they would do so.

Once, the family was to go to a swimming meet with their cousin. The pool was known for being a loud, humid, and hot place. Since this environment had the potential to make Hadden uncomfortable, the family decided not to attend. Instead, they met the cousin for ice cream after the meet. Hadden's parents did a nice job assessing the environment and were proactive and positive in making adaptations for Hadden. This resulted in Hadden not having a "meltdown."

Scratching a child's back before he goes to sleep, taking a colicky baby for a ride in a car for calming, and requesting that a very active child "run around the house" before sitting for dinner are ways of helping children regulate themselves. Other calming techniques may include pressure in the way of a light massage.

Telephone skills

Cody started perseverating when the phone rang when he was six years old. He would start flapping, for instance. He seemed to become anxious from it. As he got older, he ignored the ring. We wanted him to learn how to answer the phone. After all, he is able to speak. However, it only upset him when he would listen to the phone.

Eventually, he realized there was another person on the other end of the phone line. We showed him this by using a cell phone to call our home phone while standing in the kitchen. Cody saw that he could talk to another actual person. After this, Cody answered the phone. We told him what to say when answering the phone. He now makes phone calls to family members and at times to friends from school (although we are still working on this part).

John and Chris, Cody's parents

What happened?

Children with autism spectrum disorders have trouble making sense of their world. They feel constantly bombarded by internal and external stimuli, unlike individuals with typical sensory systems.

Making small talk is often difficult for children with autism spectrum disorders. Having to speak on the phone with others who are not present may produce some confusion. In this scenario, the telephone ringing bombarded Cody's auditory system and posed a tremendous social challenge. Even so, Cody's parents wanted him to learn how to use the phone.

Hints and tips

John and Chris came up with a creative way of solving Cody's problem with answering the phone. It is important to teach a concept, such as talking on the phone, in a simple, but clear manner. Such a method is highly recommended for educating children with autism spectrum disorders.

Getting Cody and many children to talk on the phone is often difficult. Some parents report that they make up "scripts" for their child to use when answering the phone, such as the following:

1. "Hello, this is the Griffin residence, who would you like to speak to?"

2. Wait for the person to talk.

3. "One moment please" or "I need to take a message".

This script can be taped next to the phone and used at any time by the child.

Phones can also be programmed for distinct rings to lessen the auditory stimuli. There are phones with large buttons that can accommodate pictures. Picture cues are very helpful for children with autism spectrum disorders and may come in handy during emergencies if the child has to call for emergency services.

Television and video games

> Diana likes to play video games to the exclusion of all other activities. She has difficulty making and keeping friends, and even has trouble communicating with me and my wife. I wish she would rather spend time with people, drawing, reading, or doing something beyond her games. When it is time for dinner or for bed, she has trouble turning off her games. I'm not sure what we would do if the video game system broke. I think Diana would stay in her room by herself, doing nothing. She did this at one time.
>
> James, Diana's dad

What happened?

Individuals naturally gravitate towards those activities in which they feel successful. Additionally, video games have been shown to release neurotransmitters in the brain related to pleasure. For a child who has difficulty relating to others and doing activities that are enjoyable and which are successful, video games provide not only an escape, but real pleasure. As such, video games have been used successfully as a motivator to help a child learn new skills and try new activities. We are not suggesting that social skills and academic skills be learned using video game systems, although such software is being developed. Rather, rewarding children with a reasonable amount of time with such systems has worked well for many children.

Hints and tips

Parents report having a very difficult time when they remove television or video game time from their child with an autism spectrum disorder. Such children often have difficulty understanding verbal explanations, such as why it is not good to devote most of an individual's time to these activities. Additionally, children with autism spectrum disorders often have difficulty thinking in abstract terms, for instance, when an explanation is given about how often the child can watch television.

As in many of situations presented in the book, a visual schedule is needed to help a child understand his physical environment. This includes video game or television time.

There is a great opportunity here for children who enjoy television and video games. They may be used as powerful tools for parents and carers to use to reinforce or reward appropriate behaviors. "First-then" cards, as described in Chapter 6, are visual strategies to help a child understand that "First" they perform a desirable behavior, such as brushing his teeth, "Then" they can receive a reinforce such as watching a certain amount of television. Rewarding appropriate behavior results in a repetition of the behavior.

There is yet another opportunity to use video-games to assist children with autism spectrum disorders. Video game consoles now come with multiplayer modes in which players can play in competition or in cooperation with each other. Some consoles come with headsets in which players can speak to each other. Socialization for children with autism spectrum disorders is a challenge, and many children chose to withdraw, rather than interact. Encouraging socialization using a highly extrinsically (external) rewarding activity, such as video gaming, is being used by many parents to help "connect" with their children.

Textures and temperatures

Changes in the seasons have always been a time of excitement for me. I love it when the cold fall weather begins to fill the evenings in upstate New York. It is pleasurable to go from wearing shorts and tank top to those old comfortable worn-out blue jeans and sweatshirt. They are like an old friend filled with comfort and familiarity.

This was not the way Jamie saw it. Changes in the seasons meant discomfort. When Jamie was an infant, most of his clothing was loose-fitting and made of cotton. He was comfortable with this, but when he grew older, I tried dressing him in pants and slacks with a belt, zipper, and snap. He rebelled by taking his pants off right after I would help him put them on. He would then go back to his dresser drawer and try to take out his loose-fitting cotton sweatpants.

As he grew older, he refused to wear anything except the loose-fitting cotton sweatpants. He insisted on wearing them to school, to church, and everywhere else. He would change the pants, but only to other sweatpants. When asked what he didn't like about blue jeans or khaki pants, he would say that they itch or that they hurt. Jamie was also bothered by the tags in his shirts. I would have to cut out the tags in the collar of everyone of his shirts before he would wear them. He said that these also itched or that they hurt.

When special events would take place, the restricted wardrobe was problematic. Our family has been invited to attend several weddings and has declined because Jamie just wouldn't wear appropriate clothing. I would find an occasional sore spot from his rubbing the place where a tag touched his skin.

Patty, Jamie's mom

What happened?

Patty discovered that when Jamie was very young, he was very sensitive to textures of clothing. By the time he was five years old, he would only wear soft, loose-fitting cotton sweatpants and a cotton t-shirt. To Jamie, regular clothing was perceived as painful.

Hints and tips

For the first six years of Jamie's life, Patty agreed that dressing Jamie in the loose-fitting cotton clothing was the answer for his tactile sensitivities. However, as he grew older, Patty and Larry decided that they needed to aid Jamie in increasing his tolerance for a larger variety of clothing. Patty and Larry began by purchasing soft cotton pants with an elastic waist. This allowed Jamie to wear clothes that looked mature. They then rewarded Jamie for making the effort to try the new pants.

Patty cut the labels out of shirts and pants. She made sure to pre-wash the clothing to remove the sizing that makes new clothes stiff and sometimes feel rough. Patty and Larry also employed a regimen of treatment for tactile sensitivity. This involved brushing his legs with a very soft brush and rubbing lotion on his legs. These activities increase Jamie's awareness of tactile input through his legs and decreased the sensitivity of his legs over time. The next step was to get Jamie to be able to transition from short-sleeve to long-sleeve t-shirts.

Patty bought long-sleeve shirts made of the same material as the short-sleeve t-shirts. Patty and Larry then taught Jamie how to roll up his shirt sleeves in the event that he became hot during the day. Patty and Larry realized that Jamie was not just sensitive to the feel of clothing, but when he had too much clothing on and felt hot, he was not able to find relief. Teaching him to roll his sleeves when hot provided him with control and this increased his ability to regulate his temperature. Over time, Patty and Larry gradually increased the demands on Jamie for tolerating clothing that matched the season and event.

Weather

> I grew up in the state of Iowa in an area also known as Tornado Alley. I moved away to attend college in Toronto, Canada and have not lived in Iowa since. We return to Iowa approximately once each year to visit family and friends. It is a custom of our family to watch the weather reports. Several years ago, we were watching the weather report for parts of Iowa and Kansas. It was a particularly active tornado season that summer. Our daughter Carmen was watching the program with us. She became very interested in the tornados and wanted to know all about them. Before long however, she was coming into our bedroom at night afraid that a tornado would strike our home.
>
> While watching the weather television channel, she learned that tornados accompany strong storms. While we did not usually have a problem with tornados in Toronto, every time it rained, or even became a little cloudy, Carmen would become upset and begin asking questions like, "Is a tornado coming? Where will we go? When will it get here? Are we going to die?" She would ask these questions repeatedly. It was painful to watch her in such discomfort.
>
> Jennifer, Carmen's mom

What happened?

Children with autistic spectrum disorders frequently develop fears that are exaggerated. One of the reasons for this is their trouble with language comprehension and concept formation. The child will hear and process the facts of a story, or concept, but may struggle to comprehend the concept, as in the case of Carmen and tornados. Tornados occur in a specific type of storm, but not in all storms. In this case, Carmen learned the concept of tornados and that they occur during storms. However, she over-generalized this relationship to believe that tornados occur during all storms. Carmen's misunderstanding combined with her weak ability to self-regulate and her tendency to perseverate fueled her fear of storms.

Hints and tips

Jennifer knew that she had to do something to ease Carmen's fears of severe storms and tornados. After studying the situation, she realized that while Carmen was afraid of tornados, the cause was connected to her difficulty processing the concept. This was related to her autism.

Jennifer decided to use visual materials to teach Carmen through direct instruction. She used visual diagrams to show Carmen that not all storms create tornados. She taught the definition of a tornado, gave the specific defining characteristics, provided positive examples of storms that would spin tornados, and negative examples of storms that would not spin tornados. The direct instruction was used to correct her conceptual error that was acquired because of her language processing problems. Jennifer then gave Carmen a cue to help her remember the lesson. The cue was in the form of a rhyme sung to a made-up tune: "Not all storms! Not all storms! Not all storms! Spin tornados."

Jennifer then used a shortened version of the rhyme, "Not all storms," to redirect Carmen when she began to perseverate on the topic of tornados. Then, Carmen was rewarded with a favorite treat, a big smile, a thumbs-up, and her mom saying, "Good job." As Carmen became less preoccupied with tornados and more responsive to the redirection, her mother reduced the rewards to some special time together.

2: Hygiene

Hygiene is a difficult issue for many parents and caregivers of children with autism spectrum disorders. It is important for a child to be clean and well groomed. This is not only so that such children can "fit in" with others, but for health reasons as well. Children with autism spectrum disorders often have sensory system difficulties that make hygiene activities particularly uncomfortable for them. It is our belief that you will find the suggestions in this chapter save you time and heartache in ensuring good hygiene for your child.

Bath time

> Bathing takes forever in our house because it takes so long to get Hunter into the water. He used to hate taking a bath. I think this is because he couldn't deal with half his body feeling warm (the part in the water) and the other half feeling cold. We take our time with baths with Hunter and he doesn't get upset as much any more.
>
> Jen, Hunter's mom

What happened?

Between water and air temperature differences, the bright lights of the bathroom, undressing and dressing, plus the many activities that take place during bath time, children with autism spectrum disorders not surprisingly find this time to be stressful.

Additionally, many children with autism spectrum disorders enjoy a warm bath or a hot shower but have trouble following the many procedures involved in completing these tasks. For example, a shower requires putting soap on a washcloth or in their hands, rubbing hands together or rubbing their body with the washcloth, and washing all parts of the body. In addition, it requires washing hair using one's fingers to wash the front, sides, and back of the head. For some, bathing or showering is quite difficult to do.

Hints and tips

Jen decided that it was important that bath time be added to Hunter's daily schedule. She believes that it helps to have Hunter work slowly through bath time procedures. A bath time procedure is posted on the wall and this now helps as well.

Other parents suggest having the child feel the warm bath water with his or her hands before taking off his clothes. A bath time procedure, laminated and posted in the bathroom, has been used successfully by many parents with whom we have worked. The child can see words or pictures to follow while bathing or taking a shower. The procedure (or micro schedule) for a shower may look something like the following:

1. Wet hair.

2. Put shampoo in hair and scrub hair with fingers.

3. Rinse hair.

4. Put soap in hands or washcloth.

5. Wash hands.

6. Wash arms.

7. Wash legs.

8. Wash front of body.

9. Wash back of body.

10. Rinse body.

11. Rinse washcloth and hang it up.

Such a schedule may seem overly simplistic, but for the child with an autism spectrum disorder, such a list can be the difference between a successful independent bath time and having their parents wash their child. Chapter 6 has more information about micro schedules for use during any activity.

Parents and caregivers also have suggested that bath time be done at the same time each night for familiarity. Finally, bath toys are helpful for most children. These methods take away much of the anxiety and uncertainty of the bathing experience. They also help a child to learn to be as independent as possible during bath time.

Brushing teeth

Robbie had trouble brushing his teeth. He used to say that the bristles were too hard and they tickled his gums. But he did like the tooth-paste, not eating it, but just the flavor, particularly bubble gum flavor. We also got him an electric toothbrush. We told Robbie to think about all the plaque on his teeth and just imagine the bristles scraping the plaque off. We asked him to think about this hard. Robbie tried it and it was successful. He told us he started to imagine that his teeth were in a big car wash, brushing and spraying away all the dirt and plaque. One day, he "waxed" his teeth like a car by using a towel after brushing his teeth to "polish" them.

Bonnie and Jim, Robbie's parents

What happened?

Many children with autism spectrum disorders have oral sensitivities in addition to not understanding the purpose of having to brush teeth. The mouth is one of the most sensitive parts of the human body. Nerve receptors are located in the mouth and in the nose.

Gums are often quite sensitive. Poor dental hygiene often leads to inflammation and pain in the gums. While brushing can be uncomfort-able, it is necessary that children have good oral hygiene and brush their teeth. How can they do they do this with minimal discomfort?

Hints and tips

Bonnie and Jim's methods work for several reasons. The desirable flavor distracts Robbie from the discomfort he felt from brushing. The electric toothbrush allows for more brushing movement in a shorter amount of time (many electric toothbrushes have timers). The story of comparing cleaning teeth to cleaning cars helps give purpose to the brushing activity and helps Robbie to feel like he is accomplishing something. Other suggestions by parents include using toothbrushes with shorter and softer bristles to help reduce discomfort.

Clothes

Kyle had to have all the labels cut out of his shirts. All his clothes have to be cotton. He doesn't like to wear socks. He can't tie his shoes. His shoes have to be very wide so the socks won't bind. Also, when it comes to wearing coats, the wristbands can't be elastic. They have to be loose. He can't snap or button his pants. His pants have to have an elastic waistband. His shirts have to be open enough to let his head through easily. No turtlenecks. His underwear has to be large so it will not bind him. It's hard dressing Kyle.

Susan, Kyle's mom

What happened?
Parents and caregivers have to find the type of clothing and footwear that is comfortable for their child. For children with clothing issues, meltdowns sometimes occur during dressing and undressing. Getting your child ready for school could take half the morning if not done well and with the needs of the child in mind. The clothes need to be easy to put on and take off. Susan's story shows that there are age-appropriate and comfortable clothes available to meet the sensory needs of children with autism spectrum disorders.

Hints and tips
Susan says that she gets many of her clothes online. It is easier this way to browse, rather than taking her child to the store. The fabric is specified, as is the type of waistband. In addition, sizes do not have to fit perfectly when elastic is used. Susan also says that wider size, slip-on shoes work well.

Some parents who have children with autism spectrum disorders indicate that they have purchased soft gloves that are easy to get on and off. Coats need to have a hood, as many children with autism spectrum disorders may like this rather than wearing a tight fitting hat. Boxers, rather than briefs, may help a child not to feel bound. Pajamas should also be loose and comfortable. Shoes with Velcro, rather than strings, can be helpful and even stylish. One-piece pajamas are not always comfortable for children with autism spectrum disorders.

Grooming

I am a fourth grade teacher and my son has autism. My son developed body odor about the time he was ten years old. It's interesting because I notice that my students begin to have body odor about the time they enter the fourth grade. I was told that odor is the first sign of puberty. I used to blame parents for not getting their children to wear deodorant, until I became a parent myself. I attempted to get Tyler to wear deodorant and brush his hair. But, for my child, I think the problem was more complicated because of his disability. He doesn't really see a need for brushing his hair, looking nice, or smelling okay. Why do people need to groom? This seems to be his view of things.

Lauren, Tyler's mom

What happened?
The use of deodorant requires the application of products that are often cold and sticky. The fragrance included in the product can be overwhelming. Additionally, brushing hair can feel prickly. Children will not often look in the mirror or slow down enough to do good grooming. Some children with autism spectrum disorders do not consider how they may appear to others. Sometimes, sensory issues, and a lack of the ability to take the perspective of others, result in such a child not being motivated to be well-groomed.

Hints and tips
Lauren was at a loss regarding what to do for Tyler's grooming. Other parents suggest that it is important to make the grooming experience comfortable for the child. Fragrance-free deodorant may be used to avoid overpowering the child with odors. To make the application of deodorant more comfortable, you may warm up the deodorant by running warm water over the closed container (for gels and bars of deodorant). Spray deodorant is probably a bad idea: it's cold and easily

inhaled. Wide, soft natural (boar, goat-hair) bristle hairbrushes are recommended. This helps make hair brushing less prickly.

A daily schedule should include grooming time. Additionally, a micro schedule that includes all grooming activities may be posted in the bathroom. Such a grooming schedule may look like the following:

1. Wash underarms.

2. Apply deodorant.

3. Brush teeth.

4. Comb hair.

The morning micro schedule should reflect your family's grooming routine. Some children are expected to wash more frequently, for example.

Haircuts

My wife and I didn't have the kind of money to bring our children to get haircuts regularly. In fact, when the kids were young, I cut their hair myself. It's easy to do with younger kids when the hair really hasn't grown in. It became time however to bring John to get a real haircut. You know the kind where all the hairs have some semblance of order! We set appointments for our two boys not thinking much of it. Well, John enters the hairdresser's shop and sees these strange chairs with people in them, with all sorts of things in their hair. The smell I think really threw him. It was hard to get him in the hairdresser's chair. He kept jumping out and saying that he wanted to go home.

Talking just seemed to make things worse. I think John had no clue why he was being wrapped in a black cape. I could have joked that he was being turned into a superhero, but I didn't think of it at the time. Anyhow, the hairdresser was quite patient fortunately, and was able to have him sit. She cut quickly. Then she used the electric clippers. The sound and feeling against his neck made him cry. It was several months later that John was diagnosed with Asperger Syndrome and we became educated about his condition.

Looking back, we now understand why John was so distressed by this seemingly innocuous event. We do things differently now. We explained to the hairdresser that John has a disability that makes him extremely sensitive to sounds, smells, and whatever touches him. The hairdresser seemed interested in helping. We picked a time that wasn't busy at the hairdresser's shop so that John could get a lot of attention and there were minimal distractions. The hairdresser thought it best that he not use electric trimmers as he thought the noise could bother John. He didn't wet John's hair either. He also turned the chair towards us, so John couldn't see what was happening in the mirror. Since these changes were put into place, getting John's hair cut has not been an issue.

Frank and Mary, John's parents

What happened?

Frank and Mary's story is quite typical. However, for John, it was a new activity and it was a new place. There were new people. Children with autism spectrum disorders do not do well with change. They need consistent and predictable schedules and settings. This does not mean they cannot do new things or learn new things. It just means you have to take steps in preparing children for these new situations.

John had difficulty understanding what was happening in this new environment and perhaps what was being said to him in the name of helping. A huge part of understanding what is taking place in a new environment is being able to see and interpret nonverbal environmental cues. The nonverbal cues include reading and interpreting the signs, body language, and movement in such surroundings.

John was put in a situation in which many of his senses were bombarded. His mind and body interpreted this as a sensory attack. His body perceived loud activities. He was challenged by the noxious odors from the chemicals and hair spray. People who are hypersensitive to sound and touch may not like electric hair clippers. The sound of the electric motor and the actual clipping of the hairs may be uncomfortable. If not carefully used or if they are not sharp enough, an electric clipper can also pull at the roots of the hair. This is true with plain scissors as well. No doubt the up and down movement of the hairdresser's chair added to John's feeling of disorientation.

The difficulties with new situations, struggles with understanding the environment, and sensory overload resulted in John having a stressful haircutting experience. For the typical child, getting a haircut can be a positive experience. For example, talking with the hairdresser, talking about hairstyles, and watching all that goes on in a hair salon can make such an experience stimulating. For children who have communication and sensory issues and a need for routine, the hair cutting experience can be traumatic. Fortunately, there are strategies that families can use to prepare their children for this daily living event.

Hints and tips

Frank and Mary were successful in attempting some accommodations for John. Other parents make other suggestions including reducing uncomfortable distractions. For example, ask your hairdresser to turn off the radio. Limiting talking can also help in this regard. It is good to pick a hairdresser whom you trust to tell about your child's needs. It is not always necessary to share diagnostic information about your child. However, if your child is afraid of something, tell your hairdresser about the fear. You can tell your hairdresser that your child has sensitivity to buzzing, loud, and unexpected noises, for instance.

Other suggestions from parents include scheduling a time when no one else is at the hairdresser's salon. Once the appointment is scheduled, begin working with your child in preparing them for the event. Familiarize your child with the routine including who will be there, what will happen, and what you expect the child to do.

You can make a schedule with pictures if needed. This would illustrate the appointment minute-by-minute. It would be good to share this schedule with your child and the hairdresser. Such a schedule can include the following series of activities:

1. Get in car.

2. Arrive at shop.

3. Say "Hello."

4. Sit in waiting chair with book (that you bring).

5. Listen for your name to be called.

6. Sit in hairdresser's chair.

7. Put your arms down when the cape is put on.

8. Watch the hairdresser for her or him to signal "up" or "down."

9. Watch the video that you bring (or listen to the story that your mom reads to you, preferably one with strong special interest).

10. Sit still while your hair is being cut.

11. When the hairdresser says, "Done," allow her or him to brush your cut hair off, and take the cape off.

12. Look in the mirror to see how good you look.

13. Say "Goodbye."

14. Get in the car to go to a fast-food restaurant [or a different treat].

This schedule shows the use of a video or reading a book during the haircut. These materials would be items of strong special interest for the child that you would bring from home. It also shows that before raising or lowering the chair, the hairdresser can give a warning. For example, the hairdresser could say, "chair up" while using a thumbs-up gesture.

Other suggestions from parents include:

- Have the parent sit in the hairdresser's chair and have the child sit in the parents lap.

- Explain to the hairdresser the benefits of deep pressure (massage) around the neck and back into face area prior to using the electric clippers.

- Spray water on hairdresser's hand, not directly onto the child.

- Cut hair without wetting (spraying or washing).

- Allow the child to chew candy during the haircut.

- Set a timer for a predetermined amount of time.

- Have haircuts less often. Cut the hair short to allow for extended time between cuts.

- Many parents cut hair themselves. Some find it helpful to do this while the child is asleep.

Take these suggestions with you to the hairdresser. This can serve to support you as a parent in your discussion about what your individual child needs. It will also show that you have a basis for making such requests. Professionals who are not aware of autism spectrum disorders may need or appreciate such information.

Nail clipping

Baron hated having his nails clipped. He wouldn't let his mother do it and his toenails started to grow inwards. His fingernails got long and black underneath because he likes to work on cars. I had to prepare him for the whole nail-cutting experience. He's twelve years old. I had to give him a schedule of when his nails would be cut. The schedule included the time we were going to cut the nails, the fact that he was going to have a shower before to soften his nails, that he would be watching TV while the nails were being cut, and the approximate time it would take to complete the project.

I used nail scissors as opposed to nail clippers. What ended happening with all of these activities, plus a treat for Baron of soda after the experience, was that we had a successful nail-cutting experience! After years of "trauma" and long nails, we realized that nail cutting could be a neutral event.

Margie, Baron's mom

What happened?

You would think that nail cutting is such a simple task that it would not require planning and preparation. However, since the activity deals with a potentially acute sensory experience, it is important that much care be afforded. The fingertips are a very sensitive area of the body.

Hints and tips

Some parents use a timer to illustrate to the child when the activity will be through. Margie had Baron watch TV during the nail-cutting experience. Margie also used small nail scissors rather than nail clippers. Nail clippers may look scary to some children. Additionally, nail clippers require that pressure be placed under the nail against the finger. Children feel this pressure acutely.

Parents have made other suggestions including never cutting nails too short (this may be the last time the child lets you get close to his or her nails!). One parent suggested that you do all the family members' nails on the same night so no one feels singled out.

Toilet training

Toilet training was difficult. When Bryan was about two and a half years old, we started to expose him to using the toilet. We placed him on a potty chair in the bathroom everyday for a few minutes. We tried going without diapers for about a week. This was before he was diagnosed with autism.

Bryan was not ready, so we went back to diapers full time. We attempted toilet training again a year later. Bryan was resistant to sitting on the toilet and even going into the bathroom. It turned into a power struggle. We took our concerns to Bryan's doctor who referred us to a developmental pediatrician. This pediatrician gave Bryan the diagnosis of autism. This doctor advised that we ease up on the power struggle and toilet training for now.

We allowed Bryan to stay in diapers until he was four and a half. We tried again with Bryan and he was ready. We were able to have a conversation about using the toilet and he understood what he needed to do. He also saw that other children his age were using the toilet. That was a huge help.

Bill and Kay, Bryan's parents

What happened?

To enable a child to be toilet trained, three developmental skills are needed. First, the child needs to have the receptive language skills to understand what is being asked. Second, the child has to have the physical ability to retain their wastes. Third, the child needs to have the desire to use the toilet.

The diagnostic criteria for autism include delayed language development. In Bryan's case, language was probably an issue. At the point that the power struggle was taking place, Bryan had neither the language ability nor the desire to use the toilet. He may not have even had the physical ability to retain. It is understandable that the initial attempts at toilet training were unsuccessful. Waiting was perhaps the best thing Bryan's parents could have done. Additionally, talking about toileting and having Bryan see other children of his age use the toilet was also very helpful.

Hints and tips

Several parents suggest that it is advisable to wait until a child is developmentally ready before beginning toilet training. One way to tell if a child is physically ready to use the toilet is to see if he or she has a dry diaper through the night. If a child can retain his or her wastes during the night, this may indicate the needed internal controls necessary to begin toilet training.

Some parents suggested the following method to help their child become toilet trained. It worked for them because it did not involve a lot of speaking. Verbal directions can be a distraction to children with autism spectrum disorders. To get started with toilet training, it is helpful to know roughly when your child is ready to go. When your child feels the need to "go," that is the time to bring him or her to the bathroom. Individuals usually void about twenty minutes after eating. Each child is different, so it may be necessary to chart these intervals. Timing is everything. Bring your child to the bathroom about when they are expected to have to go.

Other parents attempted to make the experience of using the bathroom less stressful and perhaps even rewarding. To make the experience understandable, a micro schedule of what people do while in the bathroom may be used. It may include phrases or drawings placed in the following order:

1. Take a book.

2. Put seat down.

3. Sit down.

4. Look at book.

5. Use toilet paper.

6. Flush.

7. Wash hands.

8. Get sticker and put on chart.

Having time to look at a book and getting stickers can be a rewarding experience. Sticker charts are a great way to build motivation towards complying with this new routine. It may help the child change his or her routine from wearing a diaper to using a toilet. Stickers can be redeemed by the child for treats that are of a strong personal interest to the child (e.g., extra time on the computer). The child can begin to associate using the bathroom with a positive experience thereby making toilet training and toileting less anxiety producing.

3: Community

How often have you seen a child in the supermarket misbehave? The sight has become common. Many parents choose not to bring their child out to such stores because the experience is so stressful. Going to the supermarket is perhaps boring to children. There's nothing to do except follow mom or dad. The child thinks, "Who knows how long we'll be here?" He or she would rather be scouting the neighborhood, playing with friends, or watching TV. Going to the store is not easy on parents either. Trying to keep their children well-behaved, looking for items on sale, and staying within the budget is difficult to do. All children need very clear limits and boundaries from their parents, and can behave within these parameters. However, for children with autism spectrum disorders, their acting out often has more to do with not knowing what to do, rather than willfully disobeying their parent.

For parents and caregivers of children with autism spectrum disorders, not only can the experience of going to the store be difficult, it can border on being traumatizing. It is one thing for a child to tantrum in the supermarket, it is quite another to have your child lie on the floor screaming, flapping or, worse, hitting others. Perhaps here is a clear example where the reader may expect other parents to recommend that their child not go to the supermarket. The opposite of this is true.

One purpose of this book is to give parents and caregivers hope and tools they can use to have their child participate in the world as other children do. We are not promising that children with autism spectrum disorders will always function better in situations as compared with their typical peers. Using the right interventions, however, parents and caregivers can expect their child with an autism spectrum disorder to do as well.

Parents and caregivers have varying degrees of knowledge regarding what it takes to help their child with an autism spectrum disorder function in the community. Indeed, some parents have particular skills in one area, such as traveling by car. They have found solutions that work to make such travel easy for the whole family. Other parents and caregivers seem to have given up hope that they will ever experience a "normal" life. However, if parents and caregivers make accommodations to a child's surroundings and teach their children appropriate skills, these families can have more successful experiences with their child in the home and community.

Airplanes

> You would have thought the plane was going to crash by the sound
> Brian made when we took off. It was like a scream, but worse. At least
> it felt that way. I was so embarrassed. Pretty much the entire flight
> was spent walking Brian around, to and from the bathroom, trying to
> watch a movie, and snacking. I guess we didn't think ahead. Brian has
> autism but is able to talk. He is able to tell us what he wants, like what
> he wants to eat.
>
> His behaviors really threw us. Brian could tell us that he was
> upset, but he wasn't able to pull himself together to be able to make it
> through the flight. I remember that day. My wife and I said that we'd
> never go anywhere with him again. We like to travel and love Brian,
> and want him to come along with us. We are looking for ways to
> make this happen, but haven't been successful so far.
>
> Walt, Brian's dad

What happened?

Many kids don't like to fly. Many adults do not like it either. You are
cooped up in a small space with strangers with little opportunity for
movement. Many children with and without autism spectrum disorders
do not like flying. It is quite understandable that an individual with
sensory system problems is going to have difficulties in such surroundings. In addition to not being able to move around, the air in many
airplanes seems stuffy, there are loud sounds, and changes in cabin
pressure. The bathrooms usually have a strong odor.

Turbulence causes the airplane to vibrate and to toss and turn. People
are pressed tightly against one another. It's difficult to adapt such surroundings for a child with an autism spectrum disorder. When Brian felt
anxious, he felt that he had to pace. When there was no room for pacing,
this further increased his anxiety.

Hints and tips

Many families choose not to fly. This is actually a reasonable accommodation. Flying really isn't for everyone. However, Brian's parents want to show him new places and to share positive experiences with them. Some parents who fly with children with autism spectrum disorders say that short flights work well. They suggest slowly exposing children to longer flights and trips. Spending time at airports taking in all the sights, sounds, and smells can be useful in acclimating children with autism spectrum disorders to airplane travel. Another suggestion we heard included taking overnight flights.

Some parents suggest booking flights on larger airplanes. Your child may appreciate the feeling of having more space. In addition, the movie screen may be bigger. Some alternatives to this might be to bring along a portable video player, favorite movies, or a handheld videogame. Chewing gum or drinking fluids help to equalize middle-ear pressure while taking off and landing.

Birthday parties

Tony is fifteen and we have yet to be able to sing "Happy Birthday" to him. When he was little, he would scream, cry, and run to his room when the cake came out and people started singing. Even hearing that song being sung to others was enough to send him running. We don't have a particular need to sing, however, we always found his response to the song to be interesting. Now, on his birthday, everyone knows not to sing "Happy Birthday." When someone is over on his birthday, like a relative we don't see too much, he will tell him or her that we don't sing "Happy Birthday." Bob and I confirm this to the relative.

Sometimes his brother will tease him on his birthday and sing a phase or two from the song. Tony usually ends this by yelling at his brother, "Shut up!" Now, we might not be allowed to sing "Happy Birthday", but he wants that white cake with vanilla frosting and all the candles.

Jill and Bob, Tony's parents

What happened?

For Tony, having "Happy Birthday" sung to him results in both external and internal stimuli hitting him at once. On an internal level, Tony feels that all attention is on him. His emotions become heightened because of this. While being the center of attention is often felt by others to be pleasurable, it is overwhelming for Tony. It may be too much of a good thing.

Externally, the candles, cake, people, and noise associated with celebrations are an awful lot for the child with an autism spectrum disorder to deal with.

What is nice about this story is that the family is not afraid to make accommodations for Tony's disability. They have accepted and adapted to Tony's "quirks." For example, his parents and siblings tell extended family members and friends about Tony's need not to hear the song "Happy Birthday" sung to him. The family does not appear at all afraid to talk about his differences. His brother may pick on him about it, but Tony knows how to stand up for himself. Kids will be kids, and will pick on each other at times.

Hints and tips

Accepting differences in children with autism spectrum disorders is critical for families. Children with autism spectrum disorders do have to conform quite a bit to the norms of society to be able to become as independent as possible. Like all individuals, becoming independent, having a job, and living away from home are major goals.

However, society should not expect individuals with autism spectrum disorders to conform to everything. Individuals with autism spectrum disorders often cannot, even with years of molding and training, act just like their "typical" counterparts. Families need to work with their children to find a balance between working on certain skills while other differences are accepted (e.g., Tony not wanting the song "Happy Birthday" sung to him). Differences are okay. Peculiarities are okay. Families can benefit from knowing that many famous and successful people were considered "different" or "unusual."

Car travel

It seemed like Mark was upset for the entire trip. Nothing we did seemed to help. A parenting magazine suggested that we have crayons, paper, and some toys to play with. Mark used these for about five minutes and became upset having to stay in the car. My parents live three hours away. We had to stop every ten minutes to let Mark out of the car. I think he really hated the seatbelt confining him to the back seat. Perhaps we could get a larger car but we can't afford one right now. We'd hate to have to stay home. Before Mark came along, we loved taking drives and visiting family and friends.

Brenda and Tom, Mark's parents

What happened?

Mark is used to having the run of the house and not being confined to small spaces. Mark does not see the benefit of having to stay in the car so long. Even though his parents explained to him the purpose of being in the car so long, Mark's poor concept of time kept him from making this connection. Yes, he would like to see grandma and grandpa, but he does not see the return on the investment of being uncomfortable. Adults can justify driving long distances because they see the end benefit. Children with autism spectrum disorders often do not make such connections. Additionally, because of their sensory needs, traveling in a car can feel truly unbearable. Cars are cramped. There is little to do. Sometimes they are quite hot and noisy. It is hard to sleep in a car. The sun is often shining brightly through the windows. Starting and stopping the car adds to the discomfort. There is no toilet in the car. You cannot stand up.

Hints and tips

While Brenda and Tom are looking for solutions to their problems, other parents have made some suggestions to make car trips more enjoyable for children with autism spectrum disorders. This is important because these children simply cannot bear being so uncomfortable for such a long time.

They need to know how a trip can benefit them and that the trip will not be uncomfortable.

Some parents say that a timer is useful for a child to see to give them visual cues regarding the abstract concept of time. The time can be set for smaller segments of time, rather than for the entire trip. At the end of each thirty minutes, the child can be given something different to do. Snacks at intervals are helpful as well. These can be given at the end of specific periods.

It is important that the child has a large choice of objects to manipulate. Small toys that can be used in confined spaces, books, and other items of interest are also helpful. These can be included in what is commonly referred to as a "wait box." Wait boxes are often used in schools with children with autism spectrum disorders because there is a lot of time that children have to wait between classes and activities. Children with autism spectrum disorders need help with such down times, like riding in a car. Chapter 6 has more information regarding wait boxes.

Some parents suggest making a map of the trip for the child to follow. The map can have pictures of landmarks and names and numbers of roads on it. It can be used in a treasure hunt sort of activity. Other parents say that they limit the amount of sugars in foods on a trip because children do not have the physical space to burn this energy off.

It is recommended that parents and caregivers try to follow the child's normal schedule regarding meals and bedtimes. It is important for a child with a sensitive sensory system to have consistency in this regard. Most of the parents we talked to say that there should be time at the end of the day, after traveling, to be left alone and to unwind. Some children need this time to run around. Many of these accommodations would work for children without autism spectrum disorders as well. The difference is that accommodations on long trips are "must do's" for children with autism spectrum disorders.

Car travel 2 - Child safety seats

We like to go to a lot of places, but Ross cannot stand to go anywhere in the car. He hates his car seat. When he was a baby, he squirmed a lot in the seat, but this was not a big problem. Around when he turned three, he began to fight getting into his seat. The sight of the car makes him cry, and I don't remember the last time we went to the store, that Ross didn't freak out trying to get him in the car. Other kids travel just fine. I know Ross has autism, but I know kids with autism that go with their moms everywhere. The seat is comfortable and I keep the air conditioning on high, since Ross hates the heat. We've tried providing snacks, movies, and other things to distract Ross. We also tried extra padding, but this didn't seem to help. Ross likes to be very active, but sometimes kids have to sit down and ride in a car. This is reality.

Kurt, Ross's dad

What happened?

While this parent might not know it, car seats present a challenge for a great many children with autism spectrum disorders. Many children with autism spectrum disorders do not like being confined into small spaces. As with many children, those with autism spectrum disorders like to run around and to be active. Given impaired sensory systems, discomfort to children with autism spectrum disorders has a pronounced effect, even if they are not actually feeling pain. Additionally, impaired executive functioning prevents many children with autism spectrum disorders from controlling their impulses, for example, the urge to run or flee.

Hints and tips

Children with autism spectrum disorders often have a heightened reaction to touch. Some children need labels removed from clothing because of the significant discomfort that these labels provide (see Chapter 1, Textures and temperatures for more information in this regard). It is interesting that Kurt believes the child safety seat to be comfortable. He adds that padding was provided to help in this regard. It is very likely that Ross is quite uncomfortable in his seat. Additionally, it is likely that Ross would appreciate less padding, and not more. Tight seating, like tight clothing, could likely have the effect of rubbing against Ross' skin. For a child with a sensory problem, this could mean excruciating discomfort, particularly for long periods of time.

To ensure comfort and safety, it is suggested that the car be heated or cooled before the child is seated. This way, the child can wear light and comfortable clothing in his child safety seat. This can likely reduce the amount of exposure to rubbing from excess clothing, such as winter coats and existing child safety seat padding. Sensory stimulation has been reported to relax children with autism spectrum disorders. "Brushing" is one example, in which a small, specialized brush is used over the child's body. Deep tissue massage is another example. These procedures have been reported by parents and professionals in helping to induce relation and resistance to skin sensitivity. This has not been proven scientifically, however.

Hotels and vacations

We went online to show Jacob the picture of the hotel in which we were going to stay. The website had pictures of the room as well. We explained what room service was. Jacob was excited to think that he could be in bed, have us call for food, and it would be delivered to us. The first thing we did when we got to the hotel was to check in and bring Jacob to the room. This way he could orient himself to his room as his basis for the visit. We gave Jacob a few drawers of his own to use and we set up his hygiene supplies in the bathroom. He had his own bed. We brought along his favorite books and toys and set these out as well. We even brought his comforter! Anyway, we had the greatest vacation.

Anne and Mike, Jacob's parents

What happened?
Children with autism spectrum disorders often experience a great deal of anxiety in unfamiliar settings. Often, screaming, perseverating, and other similar behaviors are their way of communicating to adults to say, "I don't know what to do. I don't understand where I am." Parents indicate that exposing their children to elements of a planned trip ahead of time helps to reduce anxiety and meltdowns on such trips. Jacob's experience was successful because he knew what to expect. His emotional needs to feel secure were addressed with having familiar transitional objects. Jacob did not act out. He felt comfortable.

Hints and tips
Anne and Mike did what all parents and caregivers need to do: prepare, prepare, prepare. Before leaving home, Jacob already knew where he was going, what the place looked like, and how long he was staying. In preparation for a trip, Anne and Mike exposed Jacob to every place they would sleep, the foods they would have, and a detailed schedule of the trip. Transitional objects, such as the comforter and familiar toys, are essential for helping to take the anxiety out of going away.

Play dates

Matthew doesn't have many friends. In fact, I can't really think of anyone that he would ask over to our house. Matthew is a nice kid though. He likes anyone who likes him. There is a girl in his fourth grade class that likes him as a friend. I took them to a fast-food restaurant and then they came back to the house to play. However, Matthew spent a few minutes with her and then went into his own world, looking at magazines. His friend spent time with Matthew's baby sister and me. She seemed uncomfortable after a while, so I took her home.

Kathy, Matthew's mom

What happened?
Children with autism spectrum disorders often have difficulty taking the perspective of other people. In other words, they have difficulty understanding how another person may feel or think. They often have trouble reading social cues, such as a friend's dissatisfaction with a visit. They may not realize that a friend would not enjoy a visit without interaction. Matthew probably did not understand that he needed to be engaged with his friend during a visit. It is important for children to be clear about what they need to do during play dates.

Hints and tips
Kathy could benefit from what some other parents suggest. A child with an autism spectrum disorder can be taught how to receive a visitor. When you visit a friend, you spend time with them. Otherwise, feelings can be hurt, friends may become bored, and the visit becomes not enjoyable. Some parents report that role-playing helps children with autism spectrum disorders learn how to interact with others. Role-playing helps individuals understand the perspective of other people.

In role-playing with your child, you may want to act out the role of the child being visited. You and your child can go through an activity in which there is a visit but, sadly, no one plays with each other. Then, a role-play activity is done representing a successful visit where friends are engaged in fun activities. The parent models how friends act during a successful play date.

As children become adept at playing with each other, conversational topics may be addressed. For instance, you may want to teach your child what to say on a play date. Chapter 6 provides information regarding how to role-play with your child. The sample given includes how to teach your child what to say on a play date.

In addition to role-playing, there are other activities that parents and caregivers have suggested. It often helps to set up some play activities before the play date begins. A written list of activities can be posted on the refrigerator. Stories using pictures can often help a child with an autism spectrum disorder see and remember what he or she needs to do on a play date.

Sometimes a parent may need to start the play. There is nothing wrong with a play date lasting just an hour. Perhaps this is all the time that the children can handle. Play dates can be made longer as time goes on.

Reading faces and emotions

When I took Julie to the hospital, I asked that the neighbor watch Jeffrey. I didn't realize it until afterward, but Cheryl was afraid to watch him. Jeffrey does have trouble understanding why people feel frustrated or mad at times. He often doesn't know how to respond in these situations. Sometimes he brings on frustration in people as he doesn't understand the message they are trying to send. Jeffrey had trouble at Cheryl's house and got upset. Cheryl asked him to pick a toy to play with or to watch TV. He didn't want to do either because he was hungry, but was afraid to say so. Jeffrey cried instead (rather loud in fact). Cheryl was a bit frustrated because she could not console Jeffrey. Jeffrey became even more upset. I'm not sure what I'll do the next time I need Jeffrey babysat, like if there is an emergency.

Cheryl and Mark, Jeffrey's parents

What happened?

Jeffrey was in unfamiliar surroundings, and certainly did not know Cheryl very well. Her frustration was misconstrued by Jeffrey to mean rejection. This upset Jeffrey, as it would any child. Children with autism spectrum disorders have difficulty understanding the emotions of others. They often do not "read" the faces of individuals very well. Often, children with autism spectrum disorders do not understand their own emotions and how to handle them. Problems with executive functioning, as discussed in the introduction, present innumerable problems in regard to establishing and maintaining relationships, and in responding to others emotions. Misunderstandings occur continuously.

Hints and tips

Children with autism spectrum disorders need to be taught the meanings of nonverbal communications, such as facial expressions as they relate to emotions. Most children learn such skills without much difficulty. Children with autism spectrum disorders need actual instruction in these areas as they often do not learn skills through observation, as is the case with typical children. Several effective methods are used to teach children with autism spectrum disorders how to understand their own emotions and those of others.

The following are steps in a simple strategy to teach a child with an autism spectrum disorder how to understand others' emotions:

1. Show the child a series of a few pictures of individuals with different emotions.

2. Teach the child to name each emotion.

3. Have the child demonstrate each emotion, and demonstrate the emotion yourself.

4. Add pictures of emotions and conduct these same activities, to help the child build a repertoire of emotions and their labels.

5. Begin to provide suggested verbal and nonverbal responses to seeing individuals with different emotions. For example, for "sad," teach the child to say, "Are you sad?" For frustration, perhaps the child can learn to verbalize, "What are you frustrated about?"

6. It is best to have the child demonstrate such responses, and review skills learned on an ongoing basis. More complex emotions and responses can be taught as the child gets older.

Shopping

> The last time I took Maggie shopping was on 18 February 2002. I remember the date well. There we were in the food store. Maggie wanted to get out of the cart and began to cry. I let her out and she sat on the floor screaming. Each time I picked her up, she got much louder. I was embarrassed because they know me at the food store. I know other parents go through this, but this was different.
>
> Maggie's screaming was extremely loud and could be heard throughout the store. I worried that I would be seen as a child abuser, even though I wasn't even touching Maggie. There has to be a way for me to get to the store with Maggie. I have a hard time getting a sitter, and, as she gets older, Maggie is going to need to be able to get to the store herself. The parenting magazines don't really address children with autism and taking them out to the supermarket, so I am always looking for suggestions.
>
> Kate, Maggie's mom

What happened?
Food stores can be overwhelming places for children with autism spectrum disorders. Try to put yourself in the child's shoes for one minute:

> I'm in an uncomfortable shopping cart seat and I'm held in by cold metal bars. I do not know how long I'll be stuck in this thing. There are bright lights everywhere. Mom is not paying any attention to me. I feel confused.

Perhaps these sorts of thoughts and feelings explain Maggie's behaviors.

Hints and tips
Other parents suggest that if a child must ride a shopping cart, it needs to be made more comfortable by using a small pillow or towel. Shopping during a mealtime may give you an excuse to give your child snacks during the trip. It may sound strange, but some kids like to use sunglasses, even indoors, where there are bright lights. This may particularly

help children with sensory issues. One mother said that her child began to like to go shopping when she brought along some toys to play with in the main compartment area of the shopping cart. This took up space and reduced how much she could place in the cart. However, the shopping experience became uneventful for both mother and child.

Parents also made other suggestions such as having the child place items in the shopping cart. Some parents say that they try to make a game out of shopping, like playing scavenger hunt. In fact, some have made shopping lists with built-in point systems that children can carry with them. If you think that such plans could work well with all children, you would be right.

Shoe stores

Joe was about seven. I had never taken him to the shoe store before because I had a feeling it would be very difficult for him. There are so many shoes from which to pick. He was sensitive about his feet. I wasn't looking forward to the whole situation. I was a little worried, but thought it wouldn't take too long. I already told him what it would be like. I would measure his feet at home before we left for the store. Once at the store, I would show him some shoes in his size. He would tell me what he liked. I would tell the shoe person that I'll put them on him and he can take a few steps so he can tell me how it feels.

We walked into the shoe store and I sat him down. I was nervous because they have many shoes. I walked over to the shoe rack and tried to find his size. I had my back to Joe and he started to flap. I thought it was okay because there were not a lot of people there. However, the thing I hadn't anticipated was something on the baseboard under the shoe rack. There was a make-believe mouse-hole with some text that said something about mice and shoes. Joe saw this and dove with great interest to the floor. He was fascinated by the decoration. He was lying on the floor with his head under the shoe rack and was flapping. Joe wouldn't get up. I ended up getting a pair of shoes that I thought would fit him. I had to carry Joe out of the store.

Stacey, Joe's mom

What happened?

Stacey did a nice job planning for going to the shoe store. This story shows that no matter how much preparation you make, you cannot be assured that any given experience is going to go smoothly. Unpredictability is part of raising a child with an autism spectrum disorder. Parents and caregivers need not feel guilty if an activity goes badly. Assisting children with autism spectrum disorders is not an exact science. In essence, many parents and caregivers experiment with different methods for dealing with different situations. Experimentation is needed. Failure happens and this is okay, so long as you keep on trying.

Hints and tips

Stacey says that she now orders all of Joe's shoes online. Some online stores have free shipping and liberal return policies. She suggests finding a brand that fits well and sticking with it.

Stacey believes that you should not get too anxious when people are staring at you and your child. You should not feel guilty if you have tried to make accommodations even when they fail. Experimenting is part of the game. Experience is the ultimate teacher. Fortunately, with work and repetition, and as children get older, such unpredictability will occur less frequently.

Some parents have said that massaging their child's feet is a good way to help them relax and ignore all the stimuli in the surroundings, such as at a shoe store. Go at a time when the store is not busy. Give your child something with which to fidget. Some children appreciate shoes without laces.

Sleepovers

Wayne has trouble going to bed. Usually, we put him to bed, turn out the lights, and in a short time, he is up out of his bed, playing some game, perseverating, or walking around. In the morning, he is exhausted. I have to dress him while he is half asleep. He has a friend that would like to have him over one night for a sleepover. His grandparents would also enjoy having Wayne for a few days at their home. We have not allowed this because we know how difficult this would be for Wayne.

Sarah, Wayne's mom

What happened?

Often, children with autism spectrum disorders experience a difficult time coping with daily demands, dealing with people, and handling day-to-day frustrations. There are multiple methods that parents have used to help their child get to sleep and rise in the morning (see Morning and nighttime routines, Chapter 1). The problem becomes more difficult when it involves sleeping away from the child's home and away from his parents. Additionally, an impaired sensory system often heightens a child with an autism spectrum disorder's feelings of anxiety and worry regarding a change in routine.

Hints and tips

A few parents have reported that slowly easing a child into a new situation is very helpful in preparation for new activities, such as sleepovers. Some parents have said that sleeping over with the child at their grandparent's house was a good start. Other parents offer that providing their children with transitional type objects, such as blankets from the child's bedroom, helps add a feeling of security for these children. It is also typical for parents to provide foods and snacks that their child prefers. Of course, the friend's parents must know about the child and his particular needs (e.g., disability, need for a night light).

Parents of children with autism spectrum disorders have said that they have needed to pick up their child in the middle of the night. However, this did not stop them from providing successful sleepovers at later dates. Finally, a pick-up schedule needs to be provided to the child to reduce any possible concerns regarding the length of the sleepover activity.

Swimming pools

Jonah really likes the pool. Who would have thought? At first Jonah was afraid to get in the water. He cried when he saw me go in the pool. At first, I just put his feet in the water. I made sure to bring him to a pool where the water was warm. Based on his initial reaction, I thought that Jonah would never go back in the pool. During the summer, we went to the pool almost every day. I made it my project to get Jonah in the pool without getting upset.

Actually, I like challenges, so I thought that perhaps I could even get him to swim. I wouldn't force Jonah to do anything at first, except to put his foot in the water and then go back to playing with his toys. Each time he put his foot in the water, I'd encourage him to put it in deeper. This went on for a few weeks where a little more of his body was submerged. It took the whole summer, but he finally went in the pool entirely. It got to the point where I could hold him in the water and he would try to swim!

Now, whenever he gets the chance, he wants to go swimming. It is great to see him enjoy this aspect of life. Jonah is not athletic at all. He cannot ride a bike. But he can swim! He didn't even want to learn how to ride a bike and here he is asking to take swimming lessons. Jonah has always had low muscle tone. For him to enjoy a physical activity, which can be strenuous, is great. I believe swimming will be the way that Jonah will stay fit.

Mary Kay, Jonah's mom

What happened?

Mary Kay was pleasantly surprised that she found a physical activity for Jonah that he likes. It is important that all children get physical exercise. Many children with autism spectrum disorders have poor muscle tone and coordination and need strength building activities. A great many activities that children do, like riding a bike, are difficult for children with autism spectrum disorders. It takes a great deal of thought and care to find an appropriate physical activity for a child with an autism spectrum disorder.

Hints and tips

Mary Kay experimented by trying new things with Jonah until she found an activity that worked. Mary Kay was right about attempting an activity, even though she feared her child might not like it. Children with autism spectrum disorders often have to be pushed to try new things. Mary Kay also did a good thing by slowly introducing a new activity to her son. This helped to relieve fear and anxiety in her child.

It is important that children with autism spectrum disorders have a way to build good muscle tone and coordination. Physical activity is also good for a child's sensory and motor systems. Swimming works for many children. Yoga has also been used by parents and caregivers with success as well. Some parents say that doing rudimentary yoga poses, breathing, and meditation helps their child to feel more at ease.

Visiting other families

When we got to Paul's house, Dan wouldn't get out of the car. Although he knew the family, we had never been to their house. He was also concerned because he didn't know what kind of food they would serve. Dan knew their kid, but not well. After about twenty minutes, he got out of the car. We let him stay in the car until he was comfortable to come into the house. This is an improvement. In the past, Dan would have cried and screamed about wanting to go home.

While Dan wanted to go home after an hour, he did pretty well. We now go to our friends' house all the time. When we go to a new person's house, we give Dan some extra time to be acclimated to the new situation. However, this is not needed so much anymore. Dan said to me the other day, "You know it's good to try new things." I told him that I thought he was right about that. He said that his teacher told him this. Now if I could only get him to eat his vegetables!

George, Dan's dad

What happened?
Raising children can be difficult and requires good parenting skills. For families with children with autism spectrum disorders, there are a greater number of skills needed by parents. George could have carried Dan out of the car. This probably would have led to Dan screaming and having a miserable time. In fact, everyone involved would have had a bad time. Giving Dan the extra time to get out of the car represents a way of handling children with autism spectrum disorders. Yes, they do have to adapt to family life. However, we have to give them help to accomplish this task. Having friends who understand what it takes to help a child with an autism spectrum disorder adapt to the world is invaluable.

Hints and tips
Parents say that they have found success with visits by calling their friends ahead of time to ask that they put their animals away. They have

said that they have needed to explain their child's disability to their friends. Some have even given them books to read. In some cases, friends have attended workshops related to the disability.

Many parents and caregivers say that slowly exposing their children to their friends and their houses was quite useful. For example, one parent said that she visited her friend's house several times for just a few minutes each visit. Now, they visit each other all the time with no time limits. Some parents bring along favorite toys, books, or videos.

4: Medical

The medical needs of children with autism spectrum disorders present some unique challenges for parents and caregivers. Children with autism spectrum disorders already have difficulties with their sensory system. Add potentially painful experiences such as dental fillings and first aid treatment to these children's lives and you have what amounts to be very stressful experiences. The hints and tips provided in this chapter can help the parent or caregiver by giving methods that will make related experiences more manageable for everyone involved.

Dentist and doctor visits

I couldn't believe the dentist charged me the full fee when I brought David to his appointment. David refused to lie down on the dentist chair. He didn't let the hygienist or the dentist examine him. The dentist got a quick peek at his teeth. This was before David was diagnosed with Asperger Syndrome so we couldn't really explain to the dentist why David was behaving so badly. David was about four years old at the time. We moved to a new town and needed a new dentist shortly thereafter. David was then diagnosed and we explained this to his new dentist.

His new dentist and hygienists talked through all procedures with David. They also took a lot of time to show David all the tools that they needed to use. Some humor also seemed to help. But I believe that our explanation of the diagnosis to the dental professionals really did the trick. I think that they felt like they had a special mission to help David. Autism is becoming very well known.

While people may not know what autism and Asperger Syndrome is, or how to work with kids with this problem, the dentist seemed to have a strong interest in finding out about it. In fact, the orthodontist did some research about it online before David actually came in for an appointment. It feels good when people come together to help children who need extra care.

What a world of difference this made. David was not only able to handle thorough teeth examinations, cleaning, and fluoride treatments, he went through a period of having braces on his teeth.

Joan, David's mom

What happened?

Joan's story shows the positive side of human nature. With some understanding of human differences, individuals are less afraid and more willing to take on some of the challenges of working with children with autism spectrum disorders. Joan was right to explain David's diagnosis to dental professionals. Dentistry is a helping profession, and it is not a stretch of the imagination to think that dental professionals would naturally want to help someone like David. Joan's first dentist, and perhaps Joan herself, believed that David's behaviors were quite inappropriate. In fact, before children with autism spectrum disorders are diagnosed, they are often believed to be willfully disobedient and noncompliant.

Hints and tips

Children with autism spectrum disorders are often put on strict behavior plans that include rewards and punishment. This is a mistake. Simply rewarding children for good behavior at the dentist or doctor's office probably would not have worked as well as what Joan and the dental professionals did. Children with disabilities have many anxieties relating to having trouble making sense of the world. Rewards do not always make this any easier. In fact, strict behavior programs can make behaviors worse. Structuring a child's environment was the key to David's success. Such practices are recommended for visits to any medical practitioner.

Emergencies

We have always worried about our son and emergencies. What would happen if we were separated or if one of us were incapacitated? How would a nonverbal child with autism protect himself or even let others know that he has autism? We tried practicing a number of different scenarios like a house fire, car accident, and household injury, but he didn't seem to understand what was happening or what we were doing.

We have especially been concerned if we were to have a house fire or storm thinking that our other children would risk themselves trying to save their brother Buddy. We knew that we had to come up with a plan, but how would we teach this to Buddy? For this reason, we did not approach the issue for many years. In the back of our minds, we knew that something could happen, but we didn't know how to teach him, until the day that he wondered off in an amusement park.

Buddy became interested in something he saw and walked away from us without us realizing. We were panicked beyond belief. We talked with the security guards at the amusement park and they notified employees all over the park. We told them not to try to touch Buddy or contain him, but to stand by him or walk with him until we could reach them. Thank goodness that one of the employees found him and we were able to get to him in a short period. We had to come up with a plan for emergencies.

Michel and Taylor, Buddy's parents

What happened?
Buddy's disability inhibits his ability to comprehend many aspects of daily living. He is nonverbal and can not tell anyone about himself or his condition if lost or hurt. His parents were concerned about emergencies and needed to come up with a plan to keep Buddy safe and at the same time prevent his siblings from possibly injuring themselves looking for him in the event of a home fire or natural disaster.

Hints and tips

Michel and Taylor describe the emergency plan they devised after their experience at the amusement park:

> The first step was to plan for the possibility that Buddy could wander away from the family. We decided to have him wear a bracelet that had his name, address, telephone and a few words about his autism. It was a rubber type bracelet so it was comfortable to wear and easy to see. We taught Buddy through direct instruction to show his bracelet to people when they asked his name. He would voice his name, but it wasn't always easy to understand his articulation.
>
> We practiced putting his bracelet on and offering the bracelet to others with a pleasant demeanor. He eventually was able to do this without a problem. We also worked until he would allow other people to hold his wrist to be able to read the information on the bracelet.
>
> We then designed a home fire and natural disaster plan that involved evacuating the house. We drew an evacuation plan for everyone to see and then taped it to the upstairs and downstairs walls. We placed arrows in the hallway and had practice fire drills for all of our children using the house smoke detector as a bell. At first Buddy just laid on the floor, covered his ears, and screamed. This is exactly what we thought that he would do. That is why we knew that we needed to practice. We practiced the plan repeatedly. We assigned a family meeting place. We practiced until Buddy was no longer afraid of the smoke detector alarm.
>
> We practiced until we were able to fade the red arrows from the wall and Buddy was able to walk out of the house by himself. Direct instruction with visual supports, allowed us to teach Buddy to respond at a high level of independence in an emergency.

Michel and Taylor's plan provided a great deal of relief for Buddy's siblings and his parents. Such activities are needed to ensure the safety of a great many children with autism spectrum disorders.

Emergency phone calls

We tried to explain to Jeffrey what constituted an emergency. Just approaching the topic sent him into a state of anxiety. I think we came off as being serious when we tried to explain the importance of being able to dial for emergency services, like an ambulance. Not only did Jeffrey not want to talk about emergencies, he could not bring himself to concentrate on practicing using the phone to dial for help. My husband and I thought we should teach Jeffrey how to do this. We still don't know how to approach teaching him this without getting him all upset.

Sharon, Jeffrey's mom

What happened?
Children with autism spectrum disorders often do not like unpredictability. They can also get a sense of an individual's tone (e.g., urgency, anxiety). Sharon's urgent tone that she used in impressing upon Jeffrey the need for being able to dial for help made Jeffrey uneasy. It is interesting that while many children with autism spectrum disorders have difficulty responding appropriately to interactions, they can tell if someone is angry or upset.

Hints and tips
It is important for children to know how to dial for help. To help Jeffrey learn this skill, it may have been more effective if Jeffrey was informed ahead of time that they would be working on making emergency phone calls. For example, Sharon or her husband could have explained that at a certain time in the day they were going to get together to talk about the phone. Alternatively, perhaps, they could have taken Jeffrey to a fire department and shown him the trucks. This would be followed up with a short lesson in using the phone for emergencies. These activities would reduce a child's feeling of unpredictability.

There are several facets of good instruction. The reader may believe that showing a child the phone for emergencies is enough. However, parents report that clear-cut and direct instruction is needed to teach even what most consider easy tasks for children with autism spectrum disorders. Children with autism spectrum disorders have many internal and external stimuli that they may be dealing with at any given time.

Direct instruction is useful for focusing a child on the topic at hand. Using the direct instruction format, a child with an autism spectrum disorder could benefit from instruction in all the skills needed to perform an emergency phone call. The following is a procedure (or micro schedule) for making an emergency phone call. You are encouraged to place a printout of these directions (you will need to customize these for your use) by each phone in the house:

1. Pick up telephone.

2. Dial (emergency phone numbers).

3. Wait for someone to answer the phone.

4. Say, "This is an emergency (describe the emergency)."

5. Say, "I live at (your address). My phone number is (your phone number)."

6. Wait for a response.

7. Answer questions.

As part of the direct instruction, you will want to have the child practice these skills several times. Additionally, you will want to review these skills periodically, for example, at least once per month. This will ensure that your child is able to remember how to make an emergency phone call when the need arises. Chapter 6 has more information regarding direct instruction and task analysis. A sample lesson is given about making emergency phone calls.

Immunizations

Dan and I have been very concerned about having our twin daughters Blair and Elizabeth immunized since our son was diagnosed with autism. Our pediatrician has insisted that the shots are safe for babies and necessary to keep them safe from terrible childhood diseases. Our concerns stem from programs that we have seen on television and newspaper articles that have reported a possible link between childhood immunizations and autism. What if there really is a connection? What if we immunize our twin daughters and they too become autistic?

Our physician has indicated that the vaccines are safe and that we need to get started on the series of vaccines, especially if I am planning to return to my job anytime in the next year. The twins would be in day care where they could be exposed to childhood illness.

We want to protect our daughters and the public health, but would there be a cost to our girls?

Rebecca and Dan

What happened?

The topic of immunization has received much serious discussion. The cause of autism is being investigated by researchers. A synopsis of the current research on this topic indicates that there is no conclusive evidence that immunizations cause autism. There is concern that there is a correlation between the ages for administering childhood immunizations and the ages of the onset of autism. They both often occur before the age of three. However, this correlation only means that a relationship may be present, but it does not prove or disprove that immunizations cause autism. The cause of autism is yet to be determined. This does not help families that want to protect their children with immunizations yet do not want these immunizations to cause harm.

Hints and tips

Rebecca and Dan decided to immunize their twin daughters. They asked their physician to administer the vaccines at intervals that would allow the twins to accept the immunizations and recover between each shot if such a recovery was needed, or was possible. This required a few more visits to their physician's office, but calmed their reluctance towards immunizations. This also allowed them to observe their daughters for any subtle changes if they were to occur following each immunization.

While Rebecca and Dan found a way to immunize their children in a manner that was comfortable for them, it needs to be noted that more research is needed before it can be concluded that any immunization dosage is or is not safe. It is recommended that parents and caregivers consult with their physician for guidance in this regard.

Medications

> We have been so fortunate that Scott has been such a healthy boy even though he has a significant disability called autism. He hardly ever gets colds and has not had a single ear infection, unlike his two brothers who had chronic ear infections when they were little. Our problem has been that the few times that Scott has required medication we just couldn't get him to swallow.
>
> I can remember one occasion when he became ill with a throat infection and required oral antibiotics. My husband and I both held him and put the medicine in his mouth, just to have him spit it out all over us like a water hose. We were concerned that if he did not get the full measure of his antibiotic, that he would contract an even more serious illness.
>
> Byron and Cybil, Scott's parents

What happened?

It is common for young children to refuse to take oral medication or understand the reasons for doing so. In many cases, parents will put the medication in a bottle or mix the small amount with juice or applesauce. The problem becomes more difficult with an older child who needs to take a large dose of medication and mixing medication with other fluids is not appropriate.

Scott did not understand the reasons for his needing to comply and take his medication. He also did not understand that there could be ramifications that are more serious if he did not take the medication as prescribed. Not comprehending the need to take his medication paired with his oral sensitivities made taking medicine a major issue.

Hints and tips

Byron and Cybil were able to identify two problems interfering with Scott taking his oral medication. They approached their local pharmacist and asked if anything could be done to adjust the flavor of the medication. The pharmacy had a flavoring system. They decided to ask the pharmacist for samples of the flavors that they thought Scott would like. They selected strawberry, grape, and bubble gum flavors. They dabbed a small drop of each flavor on the end of a lollipop to see which flavor Scott liked the most. Scott already like lollipops and was willing to try the flavors. He seemed to like the bubble gum flavor the most.

The next time Scott required an oral antibiotic, they had the pharmacist add bubble gum flavor. The parents then placed a dab of the flavored medicine on the tip of a lollipop. They presented this to Scott to taste. The next step they took was to take the lollipop back and give Scott the dropper with medication. Scott was able to take his medication successfully with this approach. Byron and Cybil made many supportive and reinforcing comments to recognize and reward Scott's behavior.

5: Schools and Organizations

Schools and most community organizations are used to dealing with children without disabilities. In schools in the past, children with special needs were given special education in a separate class or location. In recent years, more and more children have been included in regular education classes. Additionally, there has been a huge increase in the number of children diagnosed with autism spectrum disorders. Parents are expecting schools to include these children in regular education as well. With this influx of such children in these classes, all sorts of resources are needed to make this happen. Speech therapists, training opportunities, and other resources are needed. More excellent books on educating children with autism spectrum disorders are becoming available.

Significant skills and knowledge are needed by teachers and staff members to educate children with autism spectrum disorders. A great deal of training is needed by all professionals working with children with these diagnoses. Additionally, coordinating the delivery of instruction and related services to support children with autism spectrum disorders can be difficult. Parents are in a position to advocate for the needs of their children and to work with schools to ensure that these needs are addressed. This is no easy task. Change is difficult for everyone. The methods for dealing with children with autism spectrum disorders are unique. Professionals need to learn these new skills. Many schools are being proactive and are beginning to understand the unique needs of children with autism spectrum disorders. There is quite a way to go before all children are receiving what they need, however.

This chapter was written because of the unique demands on parents and caregivers of children with autism spectrum disorders in working with schools and community organizations in ensuring that their children receive the most appropriate treatment possible. The hints and tips in this chapter have worked for a great many families in navigating these systems.

Breaks

Most children learn to play games with their peers during breaks at school. Bobbie wants to play games at breaks, but doesn't know or follow the rules to games such as kickball. He is beginning to be left out when teams are selected. Sometimes he can play tag with others. But he often just walks around the perimeter of the playground during breaks.

Sometimes he flaps while he walks. Perhaps the teacher's assistant could work with him a bit. But I would really like him to play with the other kids. I really like Bobbie. We have developed a unique relationship. I think that he knows he can come to me when he is having a hard time, and sometimes after school, we'll play a game of checkers together. He trusts me and will try new activities with me before he would with other children. I just wish that he had some friends his age. I think they would really enjoy his company.

Perhaps if they knew what I did and that is that Bobbie can learn almost anything. They need only be patient with him and give him lots of chances and give him a break when he makes mistakes. He might not catch a ball each time, but he is getting better and better. And frankly, when I teach him something, he never forgets. The rules of the game should be easily remembered by him. He might make a terrific umpire, as he can be quite rigid when it comes to rules. Umpires need to make sure everyone follows the rules.

Julie, Bobbie's second grade teacher

What happened?

Bobbie's developmental disability manifests itself in the lack of social skills. Most children are able to learn to play with one another in a highly interactional manner. However, this developmental milestone takes longer to achieve and often requires the instruction of related skills for children with autism spectrum disorders. In Bobbie's case, he was comfortable in kindergarten and first grade playing tag and running around with others. However, in second grade, his disability became more evident. He had a difficult time interacting well with his peers in structured games. Julie is right in wanting to make Bobbie's experience of break times more beneficial. In fact, if nothing were done, Bobbie would fall farther and farther behind his peers and would be less likely to make and keep friends.

Hints and tips

Parents say that breaks could be the most useful times of the school day. Breaks provide an opportunity for children with autism spectrum disorders to learn and practice valuable social skills. Too often, breaks are unstructured. Children without autism spectrum disorders can function in this type of environment employing play and other social skills. In addition, they learn new skills by interacting with one another. Children without autism spectrum disorders can develop many skills without interference from adults. Unfortunately, this approach does not work well for children with autism spectrum disorders who are missing critical skills that would allow them to function independently in such settings.

To make breaks productive for children with autism spectrum disorders, their strengths can be used in learning new skills. This will take a commitment from staff to work with children on such skills during this time of day. For example, if a child is able to run, he can serve as a substitute during a kickball game. If a child likes to swing, he can engage in a competition with another child swinging. Teacher assistants can be a great asset during breaks and an integral part of the instructional program for children with autism spectrum disorders. School staff members need to determine what skills other children have for playing games during breaks. These skills are ones that the child with an autism spectrum disorder can begin to learn. For example, if throwing a ball is important, then throwing a ball needs to be taught to the child with an autism spectrum disorder. The same holds true for using playground equipment and learning the rules of sports. Children can be taught how to use each piece of playground equipment. Photographs can be taken of each piece of equipment and scripts can be written for proper use. The scripts can be reviewed with the child before recess each day. In some cases reviewing it on the playground when it is vacant can be quite valuable.

Bullying and teasing

Sid entered high school when he was fifteen years of age. He is a nice kid who is a on the quiet side, a little awkward, and has some learning problems. He has Asperger Syndrome. He has attended public school all of his life and has gone to school with the same students since the beginning. He has a few friends at school, but in generally he has never really "fit-in." I knew that other kids teased him in the lower grades, but it wasn't too bad and he didn't seem to be bothered by the teasing, until high school. The teasing started almost immediately. A group of boys in the high school started implying that he was homosexual. They were relentless. He could not walk down the hallway or even eat his lunch in school.

The bullies were loud and when they called out to him in the hallway everyone would look. Even the few friends he did have were getting embarrassed by the negative attention and began to withdraw from Sid. They too started to avoid him. I wouldn't have known about this except that one evening Sid told me he wanted to die. I discovered that the teasing was constant and that he felt that there really wasn't anything he could do to stop it and he couldn't take it anymore. I was mad at myself for not having noticed something sooner. His facial expressions are the same much of the time, so it is hard for me to know when he is sad. I wasn't sure what to do, but I had to do something. I was so mad that I threatened to sue the school.

Marvin, Sid's dad

What happened?

Sid was being teased and bullied relentlessly by classmates. He was unable to figure out how to solve the problem and as a result was quite depressed. Teens with autism spectrum disorders are at risk for feelings of depression and hopelessness. This happens often during adolescence when interactions with peers can become hostile and competitive.

After being threatened with a lawsuit, the school chose to address the problem aggressively by threatening expulsion of the bullies in the event that the harassment did not stop. With the help of the bullies' parents and with the threat of expulsion and litigation, the harassment stopped.

Hints and tips

Bullying and teasing is best addressed from two directions. The first is prevention. It is imperative that schools have bullying and teasing prevention programs in place including programs that teach students to appreciate and value diversity in the student population. It is also essential that adults involved in a child with a disability's life monitor the child's relations with their peers. This way, indicators of bullying and teasing can be detected and resolved early before any damage occurs.

Second, school officials must have a program of consequences in place for those who bully and tease students with disabilities. To accept the idea that teasing and bullying is normal adolescent behavior is inappropriate. Adolescence is often viewed as a time of bantering and juggling within a social hierarchy. The situation is not easily handled by those who have difficulty defending themselves. The consequences need to be significant enough to prevent or resolve cases where students are teased and bullied. In Sid's situation, the school district did not have a program in place, yet when threatened with a lawsuit they figured out how to correct the problem.

Bus rides

A kindergartener was teasing my fifth grade daughter Melissa on the bus. They sat together. Melissa ignored him and ignored him. One day, she decided to get back at him. She said something to him, something like "You're such a cute little, little boy." Melissa sat on the outside of the seat. On the same day, Melissa blocked the boy from getting out into the aisle. The boy went home and before I knew it, his mother claimed that Melissa was making advances at him. I know where she was headed with the conversation. I went ballistic. I said, "Don't go there. You are inferring that Melissa is sexually interested in your five-year-old child. I know how people talk and if I hear that you shared this story with another soul, I will sue you for trying to make my daughter look bad." It was all so embarrassing.

As upset as I was, I realized that Melissa really does need to handle social problems in better ways. We can't expect everyone to understand kids with Asperger Syndrome. Melissa has to understand that her behaviors can be misinterpreted.

Jo, Melissa's mom

What happened?
Melissa has Asperger Syndrome. In her attempts to banter with a younger child, she could not see how others would view her as being inappropriate. In fact, her behaviors were misinterpreted to be sexual in nature. Riding on a bus creates an intimate physical space often forcing individuals to have to relate rather than ignore one another. Strangers of many ages are put together in a small space. It is no wonder a large number of referrals for disciplinary action come from bus drivers.

Hints and tips
Jo decided to talk to the bus driver and requested an assigned seat for Melissa. She drove Melissa to school for two weeks until things calmed down. Parents and caregivers suggest that seating partners need to be chosen carefully. The bus driver can be told about a child's special needs.

In some cases, drivers may need to receive special training about autism spectrum disorders.

You will want to continue to educate your child about good social skills and being able to understand the effect of one's words and actions on other people. Buses are often stressful places to be. Buses make loud sounds, there are fumes from the exhaust, a bouncy ride, and temperature fluctuations.

Crowded buses often include many children talking loudly. There is no place to put your belongings. Space is cramped. We ask children to start and end their school days this way. For children with autism spectrum disorders, this is a daunting experience. Soft earplugs can help with the loud sounds. Soft earplugs still allow children to hear safety sounds. Sitting behind the bus driver will reduce the bumpy ride and lessens exposure to fumes near the back of the bus. Dressing in layers can help a child remove or add clothing to make the ride more comfortable.

Clubs

James' fifth grade teacher had a lot to learn this year regarding autism. We worked mainly through James' special education teacher whenever there was a problem or if the regular education teachers needed to do anything different. I believe the corner was turned when the homeroom teacher offered to run a club with James. James loves chess, so the teacher started a chess club. We were so happy to see that his teacher did this and that the listing of clubs sent home with parents included James as a co-director of the club. It was about that time that James decided that chess was not his "thing" anymore. Instead, he started spending his time obsessed with trading cards.

We were a little embarrassed about this given the amount of time we tried to impress on James' teachers of the special considerations he needs. Then again, children are allowed to change their minds. We laugh about this now.

Cheryl, James' mom

What happened?
Like all children, those with autism spectrum disorders can be fickle and go from one area of interest to the next. What could have been more positive about this story was if James had remained interested in chess. The club might have really worked for him. In addition, James had a teacher who was interested in working with him. It is helpful for parents to recognize that relationships cannot be forced. Not all teachers take an interest in working with children with autism spectrum disorders. For that matter, not all teachers will take an active interest in every student. Relationships can be established with any school professional if the interest and "chemistry" is right, however.

Hints and tips
Cheryl recognized the potential benefit of James' involvement in clubs at school. She was successful in getting James involved in clubs. Schools can be intimidating places for children with special needs. It is very helpful for the child to connect with a staff member who will take him or

her "under his wing." Personal relationships are incredibly important for students to develop a positive connection with school. At times we have seen even custodial staff become appropriately involved with a student and provide pointers to the student, be there at times to talk about school stressors, and to mentor the student.

Other students can also have a positive influence on children with autism spectrum disorders. In fact, given some training, other students can help a child as a "peer helper." Peer helpers can help a student get from one class to the next, help them with homework, and assist them in feeling that they are valuable members of the school community.

Evaluations

I knew in daycare that Marcie had a problem. When she entered kindergarten, her teacher said she had trouble focusing. Sometimes during morning meetings, she would cry for no reason. I got phone calls at work asking for my help. I didn't know what to do. During parent–teacher conferences, I asked the teacher if she knew if Marcie could be evaluated by a psychologist. She said that wasn't normally done in kindergarten. I pressed, and the teacher said she would do what she could. A month later, I call the teacher to find out about testing for Marcie. The teacher said that she forgot and would get right on it. A week later, I got a call from the school counselor. Finally, Marcie was tested and found to have Asperger Syndrome.

Mary, Marcie's mom

What happened?
Mary and the teacher both understood that there was a problem with Marcie. Both took a wait and see attitude about what to do. Adults begin to feel frustrated when there is a problem they cannot immediately solve. Unfortunately, a lack of knowledge delayed Marcie getting the help she needed.

Hints and tips
Evaluations are done when a problem is suspected in the development of a child. Parents and school staff need to start asking questions and formulating a plan to act on concerns about problem behaviors as soon as they become evident. Early assessment, education, and treatment of children with autism spectrum disorders are important to reduce its long-lasting effects on their lives.

Hobbies

My granddaughter Abby always seems to have so much free time. A lot of her free time is after school, on weekends, and during summer break. She is not involved in community activities like her cousins because she really struggles to get along socially and she is physically awkward and has motor problems. I am concerned that she only watches TV all day. She isn't getting adequate exercise nor is she developing interests that someday will help her connect with other people.

We thought that having a hobby would advance her understanding of the world and that it would give her something in common with other kids. It would be a good way for her to initiate conversations with others. It would also be something that would fill her time in a more productive way and provide her with some fun. The dilemma for us was finding a hobby that would do all of these things. At first, Abby wanted to have a hobby of collecting items. This seemed like a good start, but what would she do after she collected the items? We did not want her to begin hoarding things. If she would do something productive like studying such a collection, classifying things, perhaps that would be good.

Tanya, Abby's grandmother

What happened?

Abby was not involved in any community activities and her grandmother became concerned that too much of her time was wasted. She saw that having a hobby would give her something to talk about with others. The problem is how to select a hobby and how to use this hobby to enrich her life. Abby also needed a hobby that she could do occasionally on her own. Abby has fine-motor difficulties, which made the hobby selection even more difficult.

Hints and tips

Tanya considered Abby's interests and what fine-motor skills would be needed for each hobby. Tanya and Abby first looked at collecting quarters. This was of interest to Abby because she could complete a small chore and earn a quarter from her grandmother. Tanya purchased a book that Abby could place the quarters into. The quarters were of varying dates, some of them old and somewhat valuable. This hobby provided enjoyment and increased Abby's willingness to complete simple chores around the house.

However, Abby became bored with collecting quarters. The next hobby they tried was stamp collecting. Abby really liked it because she could cut the stamps off incoming letters and save those. She completed chores to earn money to purchase new stamps at the post office. She also liked the pictures on the stamps. Unfortunately, Tanya and Abby were not able to find other children interested in stamp collecting.

Lastly, Tanya showed Abby how to use her digital camera. They printed photos that she liked. Abby placed the photos in an album and then she typed a caption or scenario for each photo in the album. These albums were wonderful conversation starters. Others enjoyed looking at her photos and reading her captions. The album also gave her newfound friends insight into Abby's life. This hobby greatly expanded Abby's involvement with other people. In addition to the photo hobby, Abby also chose to continue collecting quarters and stamps. She took photos of her coin and stamp collections and added these to her photo album. Abby now wants a digital video camera, and she is earning money with chores to buy one.

Homework

> Justin always refuses to do his homework. His teachers say that he can do the work but doesn't want to. They even assign him easier work. We tried helping him. Then we tried timeout, not letting him watch TV, and other things. He stills yells and cries even when my husband tries to help him. Nothing seems to work. We get frustrated because we want Justin to do well in school. We promised his teacher that we would work with her because Justin has a disability. We feel we are letting the school down as well.
>
> Barbara, Justin's mom

What happened?

Barbara is expressing a common frustration. Perhaps Justin is trying to tell his mother and teachers something. Children with autism spectrum disorders often have a low frustration tolerance. The school day is an exhausting experience for many of these children. Often they spend their· day "holding it together" only to go home and be given more schoolwork. Though homework is not bad for children with autism spectrum disorders, it can serve to make a connection between home and school and reinforce skills learned in school. In addition, it is desirable that children with autism spectrum disorders do as many normal activities as their counterparts, albeit with needed modifications.

Hints and tips

Parents say that a schedule is often helpful with after-school activities such as homework. For example, if Justin saw a schedule that showed how much time is needed to complete his homework, he might be more willing to complete these assignments. Justin may be given five minutes of homework to start. This may be increased as he is able to handle longer amounts of time doing homework. Teachers need to adjust homework requirements to help such children succeed.

Justin's parents could have also used a first-then statement card. This would allow Justin to see that if he complies with the less desirable task of completing his homework, he would receive a desired reward. Chapter 6 has information about using first-then statement cards with homework.

Parents may need to present one part of the homework at a time. For instance, if Justin is given twenty math problems to complete, the parent may want to cover up all but one math problem at a time. Rewards are often helpful and can be phased out as the child is able to become more independent with homework.

Mental health agencies

I just attended a meeting to find an appropriate program for Timothy when he enters school. He is getting preschool services now along with speech and occupational therapy. He is diagnosed with autism and mental retardation. I feel a little bad because I didn't know that Tim could have started receiving services when he was much younger. Maybe he would be that much further ahead if his program had started sooner. I found out today at my meeting that there are also community services available for Tim. He is eligible to receive services beyond what he receives in school. There are also services for the family.

Susan, Timothy's mom

What happened?

Unfortunately, a large number of parents who have children with autism spectrum disorders do not know the many services that are available to families or to their children. For instance, in some communities, respite care is available for parents of children with severe disabilities. Family therapists and behavior therapists are provided in many areas.

Hints and tips

Susan realized the importance of knowing local resources to help children with autism spectrum disorders. Other parents who have children with autism spectrum disorders are a good resource for finding educational and community services in the community. Local autism support groups are also a valuable resource. The Autism Society of America's website has a listing of autism support groups throughout the world (www.autism-society.org). Additionally, some governments provide funds for medical care for children with disabilities. Parents and caregivers will need to do research in this regard, including checking the local phone book for community services.

Puberty and school

Bryan has become interested in girls. He's gotten into trouble at school. The other day, I received a phone call at work from his sixth grade principal. Apparently, Bryan asked a girl for a hug. She said no, and she and her friends walked away from him. Bryan followed the group, and hugged the girl from behind. I received a call from the assistant principal who suggested that the parents of the girl might want to file charges. We discussed his individualized education plan and set up a meeting. Charges were never filed, but my husband and I were frightened about this, and we get concerned that Bryan's actions will be misconstrued as harassment, stalking, or worse. We know that Bryan harbors no ill intentions towards girls, but like with other relationships, he has trouble understanding his personal boundaries.

Jane, Bryan's mom

What happened?

Children with autism spectrum disorders often have trouble discerning verbal and nonverbal communications from others. Problems with their executive functions often result in poor judgment decisions, such as touching someone who does not want to be touched. Additionally, an impaired sensory system sometimes heightens feelings brought about during puberty and other life stages. Of all the social skills needed by children in puberty, those related to appropriate boundaries are critical, both to help the student to get along with others, but even more importantly, to not get in legal or other troubles. Bryan's parents were correct about him needing personal boundaries, and this is often a problem with children with autism spectrum disorders.

Hints and tips

Most children can learn about boundaries though discussion and lecture regarding appropriate and inappropriate behaviors. Children with autism spectrum disorders need more explicit and ongoing review, to ensure that they learn this very important information.

In many instances, it is important that the child with autism spectrum disorders' peers learn about these disorders. This way, other children begin to understand the challenges and resulting behaviors of children with autism spectrum disorders. This understanding can help avoid serious misunderstandings. Such training opportunities can happen with or without the child with an autism spectrum disorder. It is important that the school communicate with the parent in this regard.

Explicit and visual instruction including appropriate and inappropriate touching needs to be given to children with autism spectrum disorders. It is important that this is reviewed periodically and likely as part of the child's school individualized education program. Modeling of appropriate proximity and touching with peers and adults has also been reported to be helpful in helping teach personal boundaries.

Some teachers have reported using a hula-hoop to demonstrate the amount of space needed between peers. For example, a student stands in the center of a hula-hoop placed on the floor. This shows the amount of space needed to be maintained.

Another concept used by parents and others is that of a "bubble." For instance, a child with an autism spectrum disorder can be given the analogy that the immediate space around him or his peers is the bubble. It is not okay to going into someone's "bubble," or personal space. Reminders to stay out of another's "bubble" are often needed.

Religious services

Robert is bored during services. He usually puts his head against my shoulder. He likes the food afterwards though. He's somewhat shy going in front of everyone at the pulpit. He usually hides behind other people or tries to get as far back as possible against the wall. Robert used to be so bored and kept asking if services were over yet. It used to be he wouldn't even set food on the stage. His Sunday school teacher worked with him, gradually getting him used to going in front of everyone. She did this by giving him rewards for first walking up the aisle and then eventually being able to go up to the pulpit. I also rewarded him with a videogame for going up there without hiding. He finally became used to going up before everyone. We are thrilled.

Sofie and Josh, Robert's parents

What happened?
Robert was able to overcome his fear of being in front of people because his parents used a gradual process in helping Robert make such growth. Children with autism spectrum disorders are sensitive to stimuli, both internal, such as fear and anxiety, and external, such as noises, tastes, and smells. While a child may feel some trepidation in standing in front of an audience, this feeling is often amplified for a child with an autism spectrum disorder. Additionally, children with autism spectrum disorders struggle with self-regulation, making it very difficult for them to manage boredom. They also have receptive language problems that make listening for extended periods very difficult. Some children with autism spectrum disorders report that when someone talks for a long time, this provokes a feeling of agitation.

Hints and tips
In this scenario, Josh and Sofie effectively used rewards in helping Robert to overcome his fear during religious services. Other parents say that combining rewards with a gentle insistence is important. Addition-

ally, parents believe that modifications must be made in the environment to help their child achieve success. This was done in Robert's case.

Other suggestions from parents and caregivers include rubbing the child's back during services. This pleasurable experience helps a child to relax. Some places offer a room in which children can go to play during lengthy services. Other places allow children to read or color during such services. Some parents say that they began bringing their children to services for a short period at first. After a while, their children could attend the entire service for the whole time with no problem.

Report cards

> We got an interim report for Mark recently. It indicated that he was having trouble in science class. He has special education for mathematics but not science. Prior to receiving this report, I had met with his special education teacher and the principal to review his special education plan and progress. At that time, no one said anything about Mark having trouble in science. My first response was to email the science teacher asking her if she was familiar with Mark's special education plan and whether she was using the accommodations recommended in the plan in her classroom. For example, the plan said that teachers needed to give Mark visuals to support classroom instruction and assistance with writing. He has Asperger Syndrome. He was upset at himself because he was failing science. The teacher said that his poor grade was the result of poor grades on his lab reports. I was upset because we received no notices that he was struggling until I received his report card. The teacher said that she didn't know that the accommodations in his special plan needed to be implemented in all of Mark's classes.
>
> Nicole, Mark's mother

What happened?
Mark had a teacher who did not realize that she was responsible for understanding Mark's educational needs and implementing the accommodations listed in his education plan. Students with autism spectrum disorders often need specific accommodations to help them succeed in school. A team of professionals in the school had already established what these special accommodations needed to be. In Mark's case, it could be that the teacher did not have adequate familiarity with his needs or had not had appropriate training.

Hints and tips
Nicole was concerned about Mark's progress in the area of science. It was good that she contacted the science teacher directly in this regard. This was a good place to begin in creating a remedy.

In order to meet the needs of all students, teachers need to work in teams with other professionals. Teachers are responsible for obtaining information about each child with whom they work. Teachers can ask former teachers and administrators for supporting information. You have the right to request from your child's teacher information that can help you help your child in school. For example, you may find it beneficial to review study materials before tests with your child. You may also want to work with your child on their homework assignments. It may be that you volunteer to help make adapted materials for your child. For example, study guides are useful for students as they summarize the main ideas in the curriculum.

Parents say that teachers may benefit from specific training regarding working with children with autism spectrum disorders. Methods for working effectively with such children are often unique. Teachers of children with autism spectrum disorders need to request such training.

School lunches

I would not believe my story if I had not lived it myself. My son Richard has always had a restricted range of foods that he will eat. He has always liked bread, cheese, and chicken. I can remember when he first tasted pizza. He loved it from the very beginning. He loved it so much that by the time he entered school at age five it was the only food he would eat for lunch. For a period of three years, he would only eat one type of pizza for lunch. I had to go to a certain restaurant each day to get the same pizza for Richard or he would not eat at school at all. After going into the restaurant day after day buying the same single pizza the restaurant manager asked me why I was buying the same pizza every day. I told him it was for my son who has autism. From that day forward the manager gave me his daily pizza free.

Madge, Richard's mom

What happened?

Many of us take for granted the significant number of skills involved in just eating lunch. However, eating is a behavior that involves many different behaviors. It also involves the olfactory, tactile, temperature, and taste senses. In addition, eating includes the sensation of being filled or hungry, the social component of mealtimes, and emotions as well. School cafeterias are challenging places for children with autism spectrum disorders. Cafeterias typically are noisy, have a lot people, and have many smells. Eating is time-limited. Lunch breaks are usually intensively social times and are often the times of the day when general school behaviors are at their worst.

For Madge to have to go to a restaurant every day to meet her child's specific wants was quite demanding of her time. One wonders if she had time to do anything else. Not only did getting a pizza each day affect Madge, but probably reinforced Richard's rigid behavior patterns. How could a parent get himself or herself in such a situation? This is easy to do. Parents want a simple solution to handling complex dietary wants and needs of children with autism spectrum disorders. In Richard's case, getting him pizza each day solved many problems. No longer did Madge have to spend time figuring out what Richard would eat or worry that he was not eating at school.

Madge was appropriately concerned with Richard's need for his daily pizza. Parents and caregivers need to understand that they have lives too. Parents and caregivers need to balance the needs of their children with their own. In Richard's case, he may have benefited from a more balanced approach anyhow. Ultimately, the delivery of his daily pizza was actually detrimental to Richard. Children with autism spectrum disorders often have rigid, ritualistic like patterns of behaviors. The reason they have such patterns of behaviors is that it makes the world more predictable. Simple adaptations to Richard's lunch routine could make Madge's and Richard's life more balanced and realistic.

Hints and tips

Madge was at a loss regarding what she could do to expand Richard's diet and decrease his dependence on lunchtime pizzas. Many parents say that a good place to begin in helping a child with an autism spectrum disorder handle the lunch period in school is to understand how difficult the setting can be.

The lunch period has to be structured in terms of time, social interactions, food choices, and seating arrangements. In terms of time management the child needs to have a school schedule that includes the lunch period. There needs to be a micro schedule that indicates what happens when in the cafeteria. Chapter 6 has more information about developing schedules for children with autism spectrum disorders. Here is a sample schedule:

1. Get in lunch line.

2. Pick up lunch.

3. Pay for lunch.

4. Sit down at assigned seat.

5. Eat lunch.

6. Talk to your neighbor.

7.   Throw trash away.

8.   Line up to return to class.

In regard to food choices, parents may choose to send lunches to school or purchase the school lunch. Many parents pack lunches for their children to ensure that there are items that they will eat.

Seating assignments are recommended, as is sitting in a part of the cafeteria with less movement and noise.

School team meetings

I sat there among ten school staff members. There were teachers, a psychologist, various therapists, and an administrator. While I believe that I am well read about my child's disability, I was quite overwhelmed by the meeting. All of the team members were quite polite and helpful. Indeed, they asked for my opinion about almost everything. I liked what they proposed for Jacob for the most part. I disagreed about how much speech therapy he should receive and noted two team members looking at each other. I wonder how I would have felt if I had more in which to disagree. Even though everyone was pleasant, meeting with so many people was intimidating. There was so much riding on that meeting.

My child's development is at stake, I thought, as I sat in the meeting. These people have to get it right. I was worried that I didn't have all the answers and that I had to trust these people with my son's life. I feel that I have to learn everything about autism possible, but I don't know if this is realistic. I feel guilty that I didn't do enough for my son when he was younger and worry that this will affect him in the future. It's all so anxiety producing.

Lucy, Jacob's mom

What happened?
It is difficult to be an objective participant in a meeting involving your own child. While most people working in schools mean well and have a great deal to offer, parents' and caregivers' input at such meetings is essential for developing appropriate educational plans.

Hints and tips
Even though Lucy has done research and understands her child's disability, facing a large group of individuals to discuss one's child is difficult to do. Additionally, Lucy believes that disagreeing in such a forum is challenging because parents are often outnumbered in school meetings.

Parents are encouraged to learn all they can about educating children with autism spectrum disorders. Read as much as possible about educating students with autism spectrum disorders. The more informa-tion you have, the better prepared you will be for important school meetings. Parents are often the guiding force in making change for their child at school. This is not an ideal situation as there are so many pressures on parents and caregivers for the child just in terms of the home and community. However, many schools are just beginning to be able to educate children with autism spectrum disorders effectively. They can benefit from the assistance of parents and caregivers.

Parents suggest that a friend be brought to school meetings. A friend can help you to make sense of all of the information presented at team meetings. You have a right to know who will attend such meetings ahead of time. Additionally, ask to have a copy of data or reports before the meeting to have time to review these. These actions help parents and caregivers understand such information. Parents and caregivers need to be contributing members of the school team.

One parent said that bringing an expert in autism spectrum disorders was the key factor in getting the school to make the changes needed. Staff members seemed to appreciate the information received from the expert. The school had a tight budget so getting a resource that was free to the school was very helpful. Sometimes a staff member's resistance to change is due to not having access to appropriate information, rather than not wanting to help the child with an autism spectrum disorder.

Support groups are available throughout the world. Additionally, there are child advocacy organizations that can help parents navigate the many school and government systems to get support for children with autism spectrum disorders.

Most parents agree that it is best to remain composed and coopera-tive when working with school teams. A collaborative approach is usually the best way to go. Several heads are better than one in making complex decisions.

Many parents have resorted to legal action to get changes made to their child's educational program. At times, this is necessary. However, many parents say that this can create hurt relationships with school staff. Gentle nudging often works quite well in getting others to see your point of view.

School trips and excursions

It was too easy for the school to say that it would be okay for Jeremy to stay back from the trip to the planetarium and movie. He was frightened of darkened spaces, so when Jeremy said he didn't want to go, his teacher called to tell me so. I really think that he needed to have experiences with his classmates, even if it made him uncomfortable sometimes. I think that if the school made some adjustments, even if they suggested that I come along, that would have been better.

Sharon, Jeremy's mom

What happened?

Children with autism spectrum disorders often have trouble with transitions and with unfamiliar environments. Jeremy was not as much afraid of the dark, as he was of a vastly different experience. Large crowds, dark spaces, unfamiliar routines, all contributed to Jeremy's desire to avoid the trip to the planetarium and movie. Many parents report that their child with an autism spectrum disorder dislikes dark spaces and crowds. Some parents say that they go on school trips to help staff, more than to help their child. Many times, school staff members do not know what to expect, or how to make simple accommodations. Sometimes, individuals are afraid that children with autism spectrum disorders will lose control, and do not want to put themselves in these types of situations.

Hints and tips

Parents and school staff who have done school trips successfully with children with autism spectrum disorders, report some key considerations in making this happen.

As in many cases described in this book, information provided in advance of an activity is critical to success for these children. Graphical information, such as showing the child photographs of the location of the field trip is often used. Additionally, a schedule, developed in advance, can be shown to the child and provided for use on the day of the trip.

Peer buddies are used very successfully on school trips. Peer buddies provide companionship and provide direction throughout the day. Sometimes, school staff members formulate a small group of students, all of whom are made aware of the child's disability and need for assistance. Most children enjoy the opportunity of helping others. The use of peer buddies is also recommended because it helps establish normative relationships, that is, child to child, rather than solely adult to child interactions in school.

Some children with autism spectrum disorders simply cannot handle the stimulation of certain trips or presentations, such as a planetarium show. It might be that the child is given a time limit in regard to how long they need to view any given presentation. School staff members have given children a time limit, such as five minutes, in which to attend a presentation. A timer is used to allay the child's anxieties about such time limits. Parents, professionals, and carers often say that they would rather encourage a child with an autism spectrum disorder to try new things than to allow the child to refuse to participate in anything in which he is not comfortable. Conversely, this has to be balanced with the need not to traumatize such children. It is reasonable for children with autism spectrum disorders not to have to attend some school trips or activities, depending on the needs of any given child.

Selecting childcare providers

My husband is self-employed and with rising healthcare costs I am returning to work full-time with a company that has healthcare benefits to cover our family's healthcare needs. All three of my children attend school so I need to find after school care for all three children. This is not really a problem for the two older children, ages eleven and nine years, but I have a number of concerns for the seven-year-old. She has autism and is nonverbal, although she does use some signs and has a communication book that she is learning to use.

I have talked to the directors at two different centers, the larger of which didn't really sound like this was something that they knew much about or were particularly interested in finding out about. The director of the smaller center said that they had some experience with children on the spectrum and would certainly give it a try. My thoughts at the time were mixed, I want to "give it a try," but what if it doesn't work and I am already in my new job, what then? I have scheduled a meeting to talk to the center director, but I am not sure what questions to ask and what information to provide.

Melinda, parent

What happened?
Melinda is facing the prospect of not being able to locate adequate childcare for her three children. Securing child care is probably the greatest concern for most working parents, but it can be particularly difficult for parents of children with disabilities. Finding a childcare center willing to admit her child with a disability is the first challenge and then finding a center capable of providing high quality care is another challenge. In Melinda's situation she has even a far greater concern since her daughter is nonverbal and not able to report problems that may occur at the center.

Hints and tips
Finding quality childcare will require time and energy. It will require locating an appropriate setting and staff to care for your child in addition

to the real possibility that you will need to provide some type of training or access to training for the carer to enable them to provide good care for your child with an autism spectrum disorder.

Begin your search by asking friends, family members and neighbors for recommended childcare settings in your area. Other sources may include the local elementary school, parent support group members, and local support group organizations.

When looking for a quality childcare setting for a child on the autism spectrum you will need to consider many different factors. There needs to be a smaller ratio between children and staff. Staff members also need to have knowledge and prior experience in working with children on the spectrum. Additionally, staff members need to be willing to receive additional training in this area. Successful interventions for students on the spectrum typically involve a team approach. Staff members need to be willing to work with other professionals and parents on an ongoing basis. The childcare program needs to be highly structured. Children need to know where they are to be and what they are expected to do. A consistent schedule is an important part of this structure. Written education and behavior plans are very important, as is tracking of progress in this area for many students on the spectrum. Some children need a crisis plan, for example, when a temper tantrum is exhibited.

Sports: Hallie's story

Hallie was going every week to watch her cousin play soccer. She and her mother would follow the team each week. She would sit on the sideline playing with her dolls and flapping. Sometimes she would get up, run around in circles, then sit back down, and flap. Between games, she would kick the ball back and forth with her cousin. She was showing good interaction with her cousin and interest in the sport. However, with her mild cerebral palsy, combined with her autism, I did not believe that she would ever play on a team. I was sad when watching her play with the ball because it reminded me of how her disability was robbing her of so many real-life experiences.

A couple of weeks later I read in my local newspaper that there was a soccer day camp for children with developmental disabilities including autism. I called the number in the paper and we attended the camp. It was a wonderful experience. Hallie developed some basic skills like trapping the ball, dribbling, kicking, and then passing. The camp worked on taking turns, physical fitness, and following directions. Now, after two years, Hallie plays on a special team against other special teams. She is now happy with this experience. And that makes me happy.

Kelsey, Hallie's mom

What happened?

Many parents of children with developmental disabilities and autism spectrum disorders assume that their children cannot participate in many typical childhood organized group activities. At times, family, friends, and community members do not help matters much in this regard. Individuals are beginning to see that with the right fit, children with disabilities can flourish in group sports. It often takes other parents to start such a group and to help a parent see the possibilities for a child with an autism spectrum disorder. Kelsey started such a group and her daughter and other children with similar disabilities continue to reap the benefits.

Hints and tips

Kelsey provided Hallie with positive sports experiences. Hallie was quite successful. No one knows what a child with an autism spectrum disorder will accomplish in the future. Indeed, one cannot tell which of the young children today will become our best leaders.

It is important, as it is with life, to never give up hope and never give up trying. Parents and caregivers need to think creatively and keep trying new things to help their children with autism spectrum disorders be successful.

Sports: John's story

John has never been drawn to group activities, and for this reason we knew very early that team sports would be out for him. The problem with this is that our entire family is athletic. My husband and I both played organized sports all of our lives. We still exercise daily. My husband bikes and I run. All of our children are involved in team sports and we so wanted John to participate in athletics like the rest of us.

We tried a kids' soccer club when he was five years old. He cooperated by dressing, going to practice, and to games. However, he just stood in the middle of the field and picked the flowers rather than running after the ball like the other children. On one occasion, the ball came in his direction and he actually stepped out of the way so that he would not be caught up in the crowd. This was not the sport for him.

We then tried T-ball and again he was cooperative by dressing and going, but he did not have the physical skills to swing a bat and hit a ball. We wanted to find something that he would like and that he would be able to do. The dilemma was finding the right activity.

Mel and Julia, John's parents

What happened?
John was diagnosed with Asperger Syndrome when he was four years old. He struggles to engage in group activities and would prefer not to make physical contact with others. He does not have good coordination that would allow him to play a competitive sport where others are depending upon his skills to win. The family needed to find a sport that would fit with John's physical and social ability and one that he would enjoy.

Hints and tips
Mel and Julia needed to examine John's abilities and his interests to find the right sport for him. They decided to begin their search in sports that are more individual than they are team oriented, although a team could

be part of the activity. They started with tennis lessons and learned very quickly that while John enjoyed hitting the ball, he did not like running or the heat involved in playing tennis outside. They decided next to try bowling. This was very successful.

The problem for the family was that bowling was an indoor activity and the family really preferred outdoor activities. How could they find a sport that John would like, was outdoors, and included being on a team? Julia thought that swimming just might be the solution. She called the local swim club and decided to enroll John and his sister in swimming lessons. During the first year of swimming lessons, they would often stay after their lesson to watch the swim team practice.

After one year of lessons, John's sister signed up to be on the community pool swim team. John continued swim lessons. After the second year of lessons and observing the swim team, he decided to join the swim team. Julia met with the swim team coaches to explain the nature of John's disability. She agreed to become a parent volunteer for the swim team. John began by swimming one event during each swim meet. Gradually, he became more comfortable with swimming competitively and increased his swimming to three events per meet. This opportunity increased his social opportunities and even allowed him to move at his own pace. He never won a race, but he improved each week. He was awarded participation ribbons for each event and was thrilled with his performance.

Teacher assistants

Jon was dependent on others for all his direction in school. The physician recommended that he have a teacher assistant during the entire school day. The school agreed and said that the assistant would help Jon with his academics and behaviors. The assistant met him to help him get on and off the bus. She sat next to Jon all day long in school.

During breaks, the assistant played with him. She helped him get to the bathroom and assisted during lunch. Virtually every minute of his day was spent with her. We thought this would be a good thing, especially because the school also thought it was a good idea. They even sent the assistant for training. However, I observed him at school a few times. He seemed not to use the skills that he knows, like saying "hi" without being asked. It's almost as if he's now helpless without his assistant. It makes me sad to think that he is less independent now than prior to starting with this assistant. I am questioning whether this is appropriate for him. If not, what do we do?

Jody, Jon's mom

What happened?

Since Jon had a disability with delayed developmental skills, his physician recommended services to help him in school. He recommended special education and a teacher assistant. The school agreed and began to provide these services.

What many professionals may not always understand is that it is easy to create dependence if too many supports are provided. In this situation, Jody discovered that Jon was becoming too dependent on his assistant and was regressing in his ability to be independent. Many children would not tolerate such interference in their school lives. For children with autism spectrum disorders, the sameness and consistency of the intervention probably relieved quite a bit of anxiety. The child gets used to having to deal with only one person.

Hints and tips

Jon's mom became appropriately concerned with her son's response to having an assistant with him at all times. Many parents have told us that they needed to question the effectiveness of interventions provided in schools. This is a healthy thing to do.

Based on Jody's concerns, the school made some changes. They chose times during the school day when they knew Jon had success independently prior to have the assistant work with him. They removed the teacher assistant from Jon, and reassigned her to other classroom duties. Jon was given a schedule for each class period to know what to do at each moment. Additionally, a system was set up in which Jon could ask for help when needed. It was the role of the teacher assistant to set up the schedule and other tools to allow him to follow cues in the classroom environment. Individuals without autism respond to such clues in the classroom. By encouraging Jon to use environmental cues, he became far less dependent on a single adult. Finally, this allowed the classroom teacher to provide direction to Jon. It is normal and appropriate for students to respond to teachers' directions.

Therapists

Madison does great with her therapist. I sent her there because she had many social troubles. One time when I was taking Madison and my friend's daughter to football practice, Madison just wouldn't leave her alone. She kept talking and picking on her. The other little girl got agitated and upset. Madison seemed oblivious that an altercation had occurred. The therapist thinks that Madison is doing well because they get along so well. In fact, the therapist wants to discontinue treating her. I suppose this sounds good except that Madison still can't make friends. Madison is good with adults, yet she can't get along with kids her own age. I think that Madison needs to learn skills that can help her make friends. She has to learn how to do it.

Margie, Madison's mom

What happened?

Therapy can help individuals feel better. It can also help them explore their thoughts. In Madison's case, she is already happy. She was referred to the therapist to help her learn to make friends. The therapy sessions did not give her the skills needed to do this, however. Madison needed to improve skills in understanding the thoughts and feelings of others, not necessarily her own thoughts and feelings. Talk therapy to address the development of social skills was a mismatch.

Hints and tips

Of the parents whose children see a therapist or psychologist, most indicated that the best experiences were with those professionals who were specific in teaching the children how to socialize. Social skills training teaches children how to communicate effectively with others. Social skills training also helps children learn about others' thoughts and feelings. Such training helps children to interpret the verbal and non-verbal communications of other people. Training in social skills is what Madison needed.

Speech therapists and other professionals can provide language skills children with autism spectrum disorders. For example, language therapy would teach conversation skills, taking turns, greetings, tone of voice, and nonverbal communication. These are considered pragmatic language skills.

Valentine's Day

Scott was never big on holidays because it meant that there would be a change in the schedule at school. Usually it meant that there would be some kind of assembly. On Valentine's Day, the teacher would send home a list of students in Scott's class. The kids were supposed to bring a Valentine's Day card for each kid (there were twenty-five kids in Scott's class). Scott would not tell me the kind of cards that he wanted. I would pick the cards hoping that he would like them. The idea was that the kids would write out the names on each of these cards. The problem was that Scott's handwriting is difficult for him to do, so for a few years I was doing Scott's cards for him. Scott became pretty disengaged from the whole process.

Jill, Scott's mom

What happened?

Sometimes adults can be too helpful for a child's good. In this case, the parent wrote out cards for Scott. This created disinterest for him in the activity. Scott may have also felt bad not being able to write out cards like other children. Parents and caregivers need to find ways to help their children help themselves. It is important that all individuals learn skills to help them become more independent. Providing too many supports can hamper this process.

Hints and tips

After recognizing the problem with taking over writing Valentine's Day cards, Jill decided to use Scott's strengths using the computer. Another parent said that her daughter likes typing on the computer better than writing. Then she prints out greetings, cuts out each greeting, and tapes these to Valentine cards. Another solution is to use a computer program to make such cards. One parent says that she has her son write Valentine's Day cards, two a day, for two weeks before Valentine's Day. By Valentine's Day, her son has all his cards filled out. Each of these methods for completing Valentine cards ensures that the child is fully invested in the process and feels good about participating.

6: Tools for Adapting the Environment for Success

A child's environment poses unique challenges for children with autism spectrum disorders. Many of the hints and tips in this book involve helping children with autism spectrum disorders to make sense of their environments. These remedies often include how to introduce new settings, experiences, and skills into a child's life. Many of the methods discussed in the various scenarios in previous chapters are detailed in this chapter.

It may be a new concept for parents and caregivers to think that they need to teach their child with an autism spectrum disorder. All parents and caregivers teach, but usually not in a direct fashion, as is the case in classrooms. Parents and caregivers explain and show children how to wash dishes, put away their clothes, and ride a bike. However, children with autism spectrum disorders need more explicit instruction in most areas of daily living because of their unique learning needs.

Teaching skills using the methods indicated in this chapter will reduce feelings of frustration for parents and caregivers. Using these methods will help children learn new skills with minimal frustration. These methods are tools that are used by educators and professionals in the field of autism with tremendous success.

Behavior plans

A good behavior plan is simple to put together. However, it should be noted that while children with autism spectrum disorders can benefit from a behavior plan, more often than not these children respond more positively to making changes to their environment. A behavior plan can supplement environmental adaptations and can consist of the "A-B-Cs."

A - Antecedent

This is the directive given by the parent or caregiver that occurs right before the response from the child. For example, Johnny is told that it is time to get ready for school. Telling Johnny that it is time to get ready for school is the antecedent.

B - Behavior

This is the response from the child that follows the antecedent, also known as the target behavior that you would like to see increased or decreased. For example, Johnny puts on his shirt and pants.

C - Consequence

This is a response from a parent or caregiver that follows the target behavior that helps to increase or decrease this behavior. For example, Johnny is allowed to play his favorite video game for fifteen minutes before school after he gets his clothes on and brushes his teeth.

It is important that the desired behavior be carefully selected before beginning a behavior plan. You need to determine if you want to increase or decrease the specific behavior. If you want to increase or maintain a certain behavior, you will then want to select a powerful reward, or reinforcer, for the "C" or consequence in the A-B-C behavior plan. If, conversely, you want to decrease or eliminate an undesirable behavior, you will want to select a consequence that is undesirable for the child.

Typically, when teaching new skills, focusing on desirable outcomes tends to be more positive and palatable for parents. In the example above, Johnny's parents chose to increase his dressing behavior by presenting a desirable consequence directly after the appropriate response from Johnny.

Choice boards

Choice boards are tools that provide children with choices for desirable activities and rewards. A child can be motivated to complete a required task by seeing the choice board in front of him or her while working. After the task is completed (such as completing homework), the child can remove the object from the board to signify his choice. Items are attached to the board using Velcro.

Rewards can include activities, items, or treats for which your child has a particular liking. You can determine what your child likes by simple observation. Likes and dislikes can also be determined by presenting certain activities, items, or treats to your child and assessing his or her interest. It is suggested that you list the activities and items that your child prefers.

Symbols representing each choice item or activity can then be prepared for the choice board. Symbols can include words, icons, photographs, drawings, or even real objects, depending on the needs of the child. If the child is able to read, the words or description of the activity or item may be used on the choice board. For children who cannot read or have difficulty understanding other types of symbols, an actual item may be used on the choice board. For example, if pretzels are preferred snack items, place an actual pretzel on the choice board (cover with plastic wrap).

You can make a choice board for any time of the day or depending on the specifics of any given situation. For example, you may want to avoid a snack on a choice board if it is used before a meal. This may ruin the child's appetite for the upcoming meal. An activity choice may be more appropriate.

Direct instruction

Direct instruction is a simple, concise, and clear method used to instruct students in any subject area. Direct instruction has been shown by researchers to be effective with students with learning difficulties. Good direct instruction teaches skills in small steps so that the child can eventually learn bigger skills. Direct instruction is a more intensive approach to teaching as it involves a great deal of interaction between the teacher and the student. It is most important that one specific identified skill or concept is focused on during any given lesson. It is important that this skill be observable and measurable.

Here is a sample lesson about learning to use the phone in an emergency:

Parent: Jon, I want to show you how to use the phone to get an ambulance here if someone is hurt. What are we going to learn now?

Child: To use the phone to call an ambulance.

Parent: That's right! Here is the phone and here is the number you will need to call when someone is hurt (the number is taped to the phone). The number says, "911." What does the number say?

Child: 911.

Parent: Great! Now let me show you how to dial 911 in an emergency. (The parent models this. The phone is unplugged for practice.) Now you try it.

Child: Okay. (The child dials 911.)

Parent: Great job! Can you practice that again?

Child: Okay. (The child dials 911 again.)

Parent: Now I want to tell you what to say to call for help on the phone. What will I show you?

Child: What to say.

Parent: Great! You say, "Someone is hurt in my house and I need help. My name is Jon Smith and I live at 333 Mercer Lane." (This message is posted next to the phone.) Now Jon, you try it.

Child: Okay. (The child repeats what his parent told him to say.)

Parent: Great! Now let's try it again.

Child: Okay. (The child repeats the emergency message.)

Parent: Great job! Now you know how to call for help when someone is hurt. We will practice this again tomorrow. Since you did such a great job, you can play your video game ten extra minutes now.

As you may see from the example, direct instruction includes some key components, such as modeling the skill for the child, giving the child a chance to demonstrate the skill, and several opportunities for practice. In addition, before the lesson starts, the parent needs to be very clear about the objective of the lesson.

Direct instruction is limited to small steps at a time. For instance, in the example above, the parent taught the child how to call for an ambulance, not the fire or police departments. These other skills can be taught at another time so as not to overwhelm the child. It is important that the child's understanding is checked frequently. Direct instruction focuses on the skill level of the child and what he or she can be reasonably expected to learn in a teaching session.

First-then statement cards

Research conducted by psychologist David Premack (1965) found that people will complete a less desired activity when they know that a preferred activity will follow. This behavioral phenomenon works for adults and children. A first-then statement card is a tool that employs this behavioral principle.

First-then statement cards are typically made from a lightweight material like cardboard or thin plastic. The card is divided into two halves. The left section of the card has the word "First" written at the top. The right half of the card has the word "Then" written at the top.

The required activity is placed in the "First" column. Velcro or tape (a white board may also be used) is used to attach symbols representing each activity. The representation may be in the form of objects, photographs, icons, or words. Initially, a child would only be required to complete a single activity in the "First" column, until the child learns the concept and purpose of the first-then statement card. The child would then select an activity to place in the "Then" column. This provides a visual reminder for the child that they are making progress towards the "Then" reward. It also shows them that they are getting closer to being finished with the less desirable activity, such as completing homework. As the child understands the format of the first-then statement card, the number of required activities may increase.

The first-then statement card needs to be viewed by the adult as an agreement or contract. When the child works hard to complete the first-then agreement, a reward should follow. The adult needs to be sure not to press the child to continue working. This will be tempting to do since the child will improve their work performance using this tool. Remember, the first-then statement card works when both the child and adult hold to the agreement.

Macro and micro schedules

Schedules are extremely useful and important for children with autism spectrum disorders. They reduce the need for spoken language and having to remember verbal directions. This also increases comprehension and improves the child's view of the environment as predictable. Children with autism spectrum disorders deal with internal and external stimuli and need help making sense of what is going on around them. Schedules help the child focus on necessary activities and improve opportunities for learning. For children who cannot read well, a picture schedule works well. For children who can comprehend that words or symbols represent certain concepts, written or icon schedules may be used.

Schedules should not include actual times, but rather, a sequence in order of events. This is because children with autism spectrum disorders often perseverate on facts, like time. The child may focus on the time (e.g., making sure they begin an activity at the exact second), rather than on performing the activity.

Macro schedules

Macro schedules generally address larger segments of the day or week. An example of such a schedule for a day is as follows:

1. Wake up.

2. Put on clothes.

3. Brush teeth.

4. Go downstairs and eat breakfast.

5. Go to the bus stop.

6. Arrive at school, go to classroom.

7. Get on bus to go home.

8. Arrive home and eat a snack.

9. Play outside on the swing set.

10. Do homework.

11. Eat dinner.

12. Watch TV.

13. Take a bath and put on pajamas.

14. Go to bed and read a book with Dad.

15. Lights out.

Micro schedules

A micro schedule is similar to a macro schedule except that it focuses on a specific activity. A micro schedule may also be shown in objects, pictures, icons, or words. The micro schedule allows the parent or caregiver to break down a specific task into small chunks. This helps the child to understand each step of the task.

As with a macro schedule, the micro schedule needs to be posted in places throughout the house that are easy to access. Some parents laminate a micro schedule and permanently place it in the shower stall. Such a shower micro schedule might look like this:

1.   Wet hair.

2.   Apply shampoo.

3.   Use fingers to massage in shampoo.

4.   Rinse shampoo.

5.   Use bar soap on your hands or washcloth and apply to:

   - face
   - arms
   - legs
   - front
   - back.

6.   Rinse self.

7.   Rinse washcloth and hang up.

8.   Turn off water.

9.   Dry self with towel.

Role-playing

Role-playing is a teaching tool that helps individuals learn how to respond in social situations. Children with autism spectrum disorders benefit from such role-playing exercises.

A sample role-playing format is given below. The example illustrates how to teach a child with an autism spectrum disorder to converse with a

friend. Your child can take the role of the friend. You would act the part
of your child. You will need to give a lot of prompts and hints to your
child to role-play new skills.

Roles would then be reversed so that your child could practice the
skill that he or she would be expected to perform in real life. It is
important that you model and explain to your child the importance of his
or her tone and nonverbal communication such as smiling, and how
close to stand to someone with whom you are conversing. Usually,
friends are excited to see each other and share smiles. Here is an example
of a role-playing activity:

Friend: (Smile) Hi.

Mark: (Smile) What do you want to play?

Friend: I have a videogame or we can go outside on the swings.
          What do you want to do?

Mark: I would like to play a videogame.

Friend: Look at these games, which one would you like to play first.

Mark: Okay, let's play this one.

Friend: That sounds like a lot of fun.

In some instances, as in the case with older children, it may be helpful to
videotape the role-playing activity. The videotape may then be viewed
by the parent and child for additional practice.

Scripting

Scripts can be used to teach children with autism spectrum disorders to
expand their expressive language and social skills. Learning social skills
can take place within the context of a script.

Here is a sample script regarding appropriate school bus behaviors:

I want to tell you about a neat kid named Nick. He rides the
school bus to school each day. Each day he waits in line at the bus
stop. The bus arrives and he gets on the bus. He goes right to his
assigned seat. He sits there during the whole ride and never
stands up until he gets to school.

Nick sits next to Sarah and talks to her. He talks to her about
his favorite things about school. Sometimes he tells her how hard
his math class is. When the school bus stops at the school, he
waits for the bus driver to say it is time to get off the bus. When
the bus driver says this, Nick stands up and walks off the bus.

Sometimes he says "Bye" to the bus driver. He walks to his classroom and gets ready for his school day.

Developing scripts is easy to do and quite beneficial for children with autism spectrum disorders. You can be as creative as you like in putting into words problematic situations that you know your child will face. Parents indicate that it is good to repeat the use of these scripts many times. In this way, the child remembers better what he or she needs to do during difficult times.

Symbol communication systems

Symbol communication systems are used to provide visual cues for children with autism spectrum disorders. Such children have difficulty with the distractions of verbal directions due to deficits in receptive language processing, concept formation, auditory short-term memory, and attention span. Repeated directions presented to these children often leads to their frustration, defiance, and lack of compliance.

Symbol communication systems are a great teaching tool for parents and teachers. It is critical to select the right system for your child's developmental and cognitive level. Symbols can include actual objects, photographs, drawings, and words. Symbol systems include icons. These are standard published illustrations representing language. For example, icons are used in formulating sentences and show all language concepts and vocabulary (Mayer-Johnson 2004).

Parents can use symbols in all aspects of the child's life, for example, in daily schedules, teaching specific tasks, giving choices, prompting verbal language responses, and virtually everywhere that typical language would be used. The use of symbols is not a step backwards for a child. It increases the likelihood that they understand what is expected and increases the chances for success in all areas of living.

Autism often manifests itself as a lack of understanding. Unusual behaviors are often a result of not recognizing what is appropriate for a given situation or even being able to understand how to express themselves. For example, flapping may be viewed as being done because a child exhibiting such behaviors does not understand other ways of regulating his or her body.

Parents are recommended to use any sort of symbol or nonverbal communication as much as possible. Verbal instruction should not be used exclusively, especially when a child is upset, or in new situations.

Most poor behaviors are preventable. The use of nonverbal symbol cues and support are extremely effective with children with autism spectrum disorders to reduce confusion about a situation.

Which symbol communication system do you use? This depends on a child's readiness. Very young children may need objects to represent an activity. Small toys, such as a car, can be used to tell the child that it is time to get in the car.

As children mature, less concrete objects may be used. For example, photographs are effective. Some parents show a photograph of school to tell the child that it is time to get ready for school.

The use of icons would be the next step that can be used as children develop. Some parents and many teachers provide their children with a "book" of such icons. Velcro is used to attach icons to a communication book. The book is usually homemade. This book can be carried with the child from home to the community and to school. Additionally, a book can be made for individual activities, like having dinner. For instance, an icon can be available for each part of dinner. The main course icon is replaced by a dessert icon as the child goes through dinner.

When children learn to read, a text-based schedule may be used. Many adults use weekly planners, so why not children? Parents are encouraged to use their creativity in using symbol communication systems to meet the unique needs of their child.

Task analysis

For individuals with autism spectrum disorders, everyday activities can seem quite complicated. Brushing teeth seems like a simple task. However, brushing teeth is comprised of many smaller skills including:

1. Pick up toothbrush.

2. Rinse toothbrush.

3. Apply toothpaste to toothbrush.

4. Make a side-to-side or up-and-down movement against the teeth.

5. Rinse toothbrush.

6. Rinse mouth.

The listing of these sub-skills is considered a task analysis. Tasks can be analyzed and broken down into their smaller compartments. A task analysis is needed usually when an individual has difficulty learning a new skill. Additionally, these sub-skills are targeted in direct instruction.

Parents and caregivers are recommended to analyze tasks that the child needs to do when frustration is observed. By breaking tasks down to smaller parts, and teaching these smaller skills, a child with an autism spectrum disorder, or perhaps any child for that matter, can learn new skills with a minimum of frustration and upset. For example, you may have a child that will get upset if asked to "wash his dish." However, not only may the task not be enjoyable, your child may feel frustrated. He or she may not know how to wash the dish. If you teach him or her the steps in washing the dish and provide visual cues, the chance of a successful experience is much greater.

Wait boxes

Wait boxes are handy tools used for many. It is essentially a select group of items placed in a box, bag, or basket that a child likes to read or use. These items are made available to the child during wait times. There are numerous times in our lives that we need to wait, for example, while riding in a car, waiting in line, and waiting for a baseball game to start. The act of waiting can be difficult for many children with autism spectrum disorders and it is our job to make this time tolerable for them.

Wait boxes can be customized for the child or for the location. For instance, while waiting for a baseball game to start, a small ball can be squeezed and serve as an appropriate fidget. In the car, several books or small cars can be part of a wait box.

Conclusion

The recommendations made in this book can be used in the home, community, and in schools. You are encouraged to share these strategies with appropriate individuals with whom your child works.

It is the authors' strongest belief that we owe it to children with autism spectrum disorders to help them make sense of our world: to make the illogical logical and to make the overwhelming bearable. It is also our belief that children with autism spectrum disorders are gifts. They force others to question why things are so. Why is it that when children fight with each other this is considered normal, while a child with autism spectrum disorder is considered strange for spitting? Why cannot individuals with autism spectrum disorders flap in public, yet a classmate gets away with being rude and bossy? These are the kinds of questions that children with autism spectrum disorders sometimes ask. They are also questions that we need to ask ourselves.

References

American Psychiatric Association (1994) *Diagnostic And Statistical Manual of Mental Disorders* (4th edn). Washington, DC: American Psychiatric Association.

Attwood, T. (2007) *The Complete Guide to Asperger's Syndrome*. London: Jessica Kingsley Publishers.

Baron-Cohen, S. (1989) "The autistic child's theory of mind: A case of specific developmental delay." *Journal of Child Psychology and Psychiatry 30*, 285–297.

Gray, C. (1994) *Comic Book Conversations*. Arlington, TX: Future Horizons.

Gray, C. (2000) *The New Social Stories Book* (2nd edn). Arlington, TX: Future Horizons.

Mayer-Johnson, L. L. C. (2004) *Writing with Symbols 2000* (Version 2.5) [computer software]. Solana Beach, CA: Mayer-Johnson, L. L. C.

Premack, D. (1965) "Reinforcement theory." In D. Levine (ed.) *Nebraska Symposium on Motivation*. Lincoln: University of Nebraska Press.